SEOUL '88

XXIVTH OLYMPIC GAMES SEOUL MCMLXXXVIII
THE OFFICIAL BOOK OF THE GAMES OF THE XXIVTH OLYMPIAD

L'88

THE OFFICIAL
BOOK OF
THE GAMES OF
THE XXIVTH OLYMPIAD

HARMONY AND
PROGRESS

Collins
8 Grafton Street, London W1
1988

CONTENTS

SEOUL

I AM VERY PLEASED THAT THE OLYMPIC GAMES OF SEOUL FINISHED SUCCESSFULLY WITH SPECTACULAR RESULTS, BEFITTING THE WORLD'S GREATEST SPORTING FESTIVAL. I BELIEVE THAT THESE MAGNIFICENT GAMES COULD HAVE BEEN POSSIBLE ONLY WITH THE EFFICIENT EXECUTION BY ITS CITIZENS OF THE RESPONSIBILITY OF BEING THE HOST COUNTRY, AS WELL AS WITH THE CO-OPERATION AND SUPPORT OF THE PEOPLE OF THE WORLD. I WOULD LIKE SINCERELY TO EXPRESS MY DEEPEST THANKS AND CONGRATULATIONS TO ALL INVOLVED IN THIS WONDERFUL FESTIVAL. THE OLYMPIC GAMES OF SEOUL HAVE BEEN JUDGED BY SOME AS THE MOST SUCCESSFUL

AND HARMONIOUS EVER, AND HAVE OPENED A NEW ERA IN OLY STANDARDS, BOTH IN SPORT AND EVENTS, AND IN TECHNICAL OPER THEREFORE WE BELIEVE THAT THIS BOOK WILL HELP PEOPLE BETTER STAND THESE GAMES BY OBSERVI CORDING THEM IN DETAIL. I HO OFFICIAL BOOK WILL HELP COM THROUGHOUT THE WORLD THE THE OLYMPIC GAMES IN SEOUL.

ARE SAID TO MPIC CULTURAL ATION. OFFICIAL TO UNDER NG AND RE PE THAT THIS MUNICATE REALITY OF

PARK SEH-JIK

PRESIDENT OF THE SEOUL OLYMPIC ORGANIZING COMMITTEE

A ALMOST UNIVERSAL GAMES; THE ALL-TIME RECORD PARTICIPATION OF 160 DELEGATIONS FROM FIVE CONTINENTS; AN UNPRECEDENTED NUMBER OF ATHLETES, OFFICIALS AND MEDIA REPRESENTATIVES; A SIGNIFICANT NUMBER OF WORLDu RECORDS BEATEN; A FEW STRIKING DOPING-RELATED DISQUALIFICATIONS, DECIDED ON UNHESITATINGLY BY THE INTERNATIONAL OLYMPIC COMMITTEE: THE GAMES OF THE XXIVTH OLYMPIAD IN SEOUL 1988 WERE ALL THIS. BUT ALSO MUCH MORE, AND FAR GREATER. THESE GAMES WERE THE ATHLETES, LEFT TO THEMSELVES AT THE MOMENT OF COMPETITION, HAVING TO FACE UP TO THEIR RESPONSIBILITIES, OVERCOME THEIR GRIEF, ACCEPT SETBACKS AND MISTAKES, OR SAVOUR THE MOMENT OF TRIUMPH. THEY WERE THE TENS OF THOUSANDS OF PEOPLE WHO WORKED UNSTINTINGLY FOR SEVEN YEARS TO ENSURE EVERYTHING WAS READY IN TIME FOR THE FESTIVAL TO RUN SMOOTHLY, WITHOUT PROBLEMS OR DIFFICULTIES. THEY WERE THE KOREAN PEOPLE, MOBILIZED TO WELCOME THE WORLD WITH INCONTESTABLE HOSPITALITY, DEVOTING ALL THEIR ENERGIES TO HONORING THE LAND OF THE MORNING CALM. THEY WERE THOSE THOUSANDS OF SPECIAL MOMENTS, MOMENTS OF JOY OR SADNESS, GRIEF OR SATISFACTION, VICTORY OR DEFEAT, WHICH GIVE EACH SET OF OLYMPIC GAMES THEIR OWN PARTICULAR CHARACTER; IDENTICAL YET DIFFERENT. HERE THEN, LIES THE

RESPONSIBILITY OF THE CHRONICLER, JOURNALIST OR AUTHOR, THE PHOTOGRAPHER OR ARTIST ... EACH HAS THE TASK OF CAPTURING FOR ALL THE UNIQUE FLAVOR, THE PARTICULAR IMPRESSIONS, THE STORIES WHICH WILL DETERMINE, FOR EVER, THE IMAGE THAT WILL BE RETAINED FROM THESE GAMES. SUCH WAS THE INTENTION BEHIND THE IOC'S IDEA TO PRODUCE THIS WORK. WE HOPE SINCERELY THAT YOU WILL LIKE THE RESULT SINCE AT THE END OF THE DAY IT IS YOU, THE READER, WHO HAS THE LAST WORD, THE FINAL SAY, IN LOOKING AHEAD TO FUTURE OLYMPIADS.

JUAN ANTONIO SAMARANCH

IOC PRESIDENT

OLYMPIC

The Games of the XXIVth Olympiad opened a door on to a relatively unknown people, whose response to being discovered was as refreshingly welcoming as the scent of a summer flower. The world suddenly found the Republic of Korea, and was enchanted.

No city has ever done more than Seoul to greet an army of foreigners, with whom it had a mutual unfamiliarity. Flags, balloons and bonhomie filled the streets. Pause on a side-walk for a moment, and three people would jump forward to ask if you needed assistance. Wave unavailingly for a

CITY

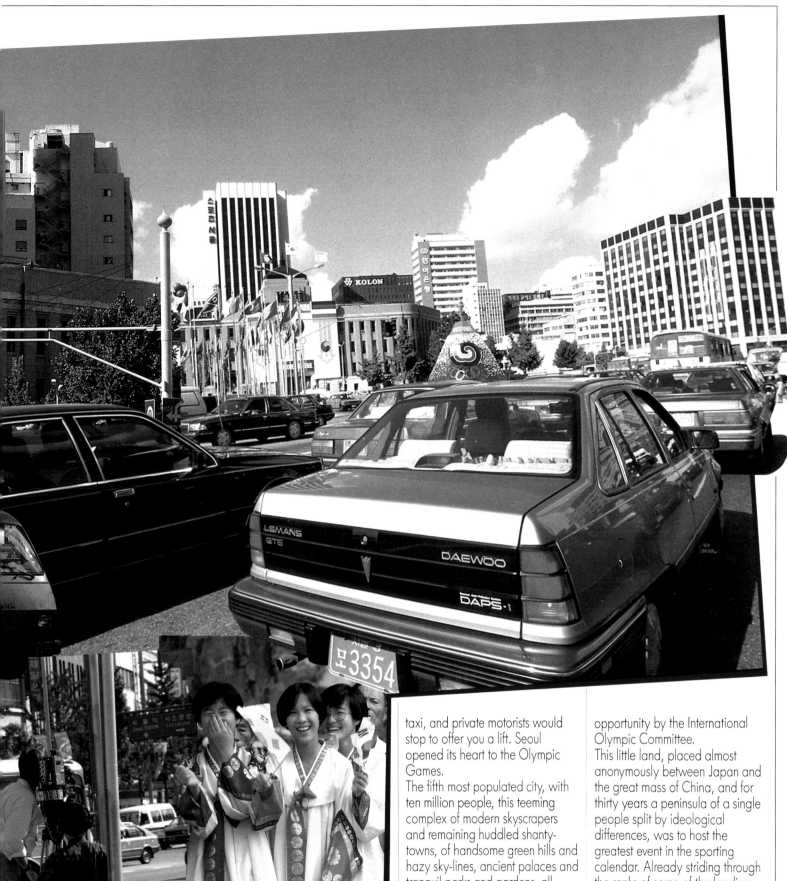

taxi, and private motorists would stop to offer you a lift. Seoul opened its heart to the Olympic Games.

The fifth most populated city, with ten million people, this teeming complex of modern skyscrapers and remaining huddled shanty-towns, of handsome green hills and hazy sky-lines, ancient palaces and tranquil parks and gardens, all woven alongside the wide and winding Han River, is breathtaking to behold for the visitor. As for the sporting facilities, the last word in modern technology and design, they are, simply, an astonishment. Applying in 1981, at a time when few cities wanted the Games because they had been kidnapped by politics, terrorism and soaring costs, Seoul was granted the

opportunity by the International Olympic Committee.

This little land, placed almost anonymously between Japan and the great mass of China, and for thirty years a peninsula of a single people split by ideological differences, was to host the greatest event in the sporting calendar. Already striding through the ranks of some of the leading industrial nations, the Koreans, their history, their culture and their phenomenal energy would be exposed by television to the eye of the world in a way a million television commercials could never achieve. It was to be expected that their northern neighbors, fellow members of the Olympic community, would be envious.

11

ultimately gave the Olympic Games of 1988 not a platform of fear but a festival of glorious re-unification.

We may have been surrounded by thousands of police and by the necessity of constant checks on identity and hand-baggage, but this is the price of a violence that can rear its head in any continent.

For four years, between the Games of Los Angeles and Seoul, there was the fear that the refusal of Democratic People's Republic Korea to take part would lead to yet another boycott; but, to a sigh of global relief, the socialist countries decided that the interests of sporting and social harmony were paramount. Seoul, which had lived on a knife edge of anxiety,

Not once did I hear a harsh word from a security guard or a visitor. Seoul and its guests were bonded by pervasive goodwill.

That the XXIVth Games should have taken place was to a large extent due to the diplomacy of Juan Antonio Samaranch, the president of the IOC. Yet they would not have been possible without the determination of the Korean people who showed, in Seoul in September, 1988, that they had the will to succeed. As Mr. Samaranch said in his opening address to the 94th Session before the Games: "I find it re-assuring to see the truly extraordinary developments in this part of the world. I do not feel it would be presumptuous to think that we (the Olympic Movement) have contributed to this."

Yet, for two weeks, undoubtedly, Seoul helped to make the world seem a better place.

It may be some years before we are fully able to judge the impact of the Olympic Games upon this city which for so long has been the heart-beat of a troubled region.

15

HARMONY AND PROGRESS

COLOR

SOUVENIR

It is only three short stops on the train from sporting enthusiasm to patriotism, and from there via nationalism to xenophobia. The Olympic Games are conspicuous for the first two. Some would say they have too much of the third. What is unarguable, however, is that the Games educate people against any tendency towards the last. The Games exposes the world to the world, creates friendship where there was previously unfamiliarity, embraces people of all shades. George Orwell, the author of the then futuristic political novel "1984", is well known for having said that international sport is an unfailing cause of ill-will. That it is so sometimes is undeniable, but what distinguishes the Olympic Games is its historic sense of dignity and nobility of purpose.

Those two objectives may be as frail as are most human ambitions, yet they are perceived by the people of all nationalities to be inseparable from the Olympic concept.

However much the Games may be tarnished by the forces of nationalism, individual selfishness, aggressive professionalism or commercialism — a danger for the IOC itself, against which it must guard as it seeks financial security — the spirit that is ignited in all nations by the Olympic flame is inextinguishable. When Sohn Kee-chung, the 76-year-old marathon champion, ran into the stadium with the torch at the Opening Ceremony, no sensitive person could have remained unmoved.

SYMBOLS

LUMP IN THE THROAT

When Yun Tae-ung, born the day Seoul was granted the Games, ran alone into the centre of the arena with his hoop, there cannot have been a mother or father, a son or daughter, or whatever nationality, who did not have a lump in the throat.

It was no empty sophism by some impersonal official when Juan Antonio Samaranch said in his opening address of the Games: "Peace and understanding are whishes shared by many around the world. Let me thank you all, athletes, officials, media representatives and spectators, both here and at home, for the part

JOY

you have played in making the Olympic Movement one of the most effective forces in this regard." Of course the Games encourage patriotism, never mind that Dr. Johnson, an English writer of the last century, wrote that "patriotism is the last refuge of a scoundrel." When there are tears in the eyes of a medal winner, it may be the sheer sense of belonging to some special experience which is profound yet intangible, and will remain for the rest of the athlete's life.

The Olympic Games may generate intense rivalries, but it also creates friendships that endure for years, among officials and spectators as well as competitors. I was on the fringe of an Olympic Football team thirty years ago, and the experiences remain as valuable today as they were then.

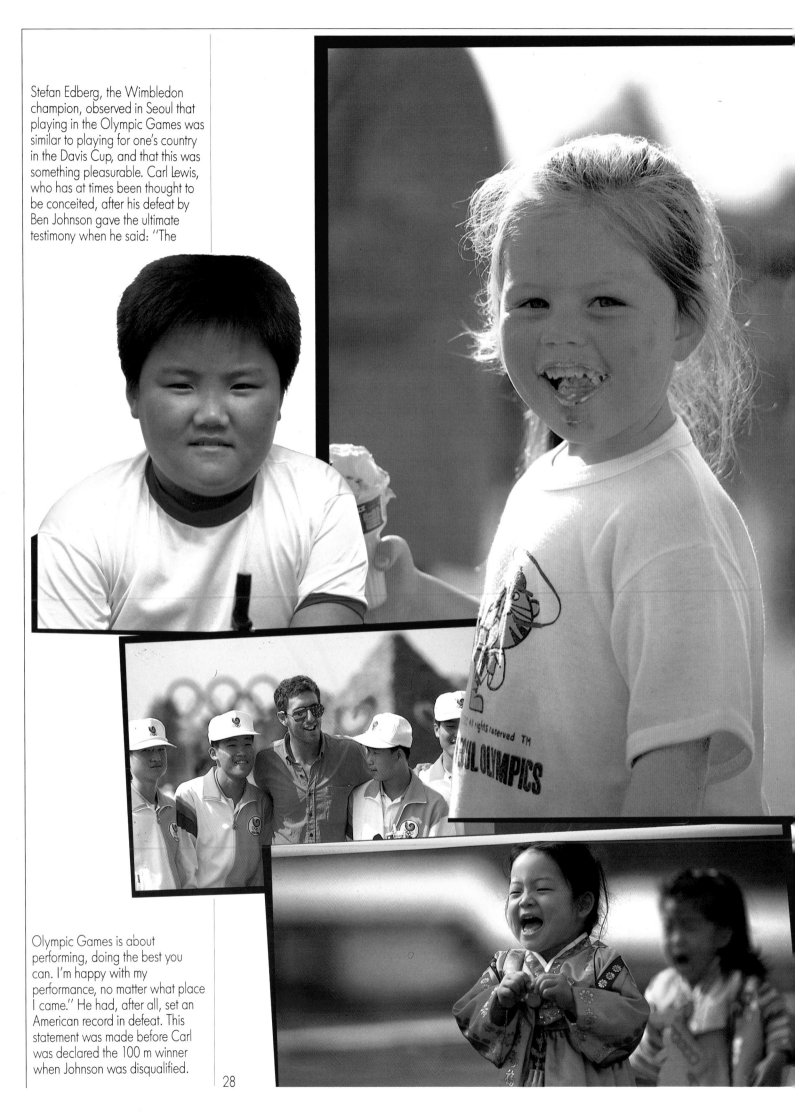

Stefan Edberg, the Wimbledon champion, observed in Seoul that playing in the Olympic Games was similar to playing for one's country in the Davis Cup, and that this was something pleasurable. Carl Lewis, who has at times been thought to be conceited, after his defeat by Ben Johnson gave the ultimate testimony when he said: "The

Olympic Games is about performing, doing the best you can. I'm happy with my performance, no matter what place I came." He had, after all, set an American record in defeat. This statement was made before Carl was declared the 100 m winner when Johnson was disqualified.

Being there, doing as well as you can, is still what counts, even in the age of professionalism. Being there is what brought 1,000 participants from 48 countries, aged between 18 and 22, to the Seoul Olympic Youth Camp; an idea begun in 1912 by King Gustav V of Sweden, who arranged for 1,500 Boy Scouts to hold a Jamboree during the Games in Stockholm. Since the 1952 Games in Helsinki, the youth camp has been an important goodwill event. During the Camp period, about half those attending were to stay at the homes of Korean families.

The experience of being hosts to the world is as beneficial to them as it is to their guests. The Korean deeply lamented the incident in boxing which brought temporary discredit upon them. Yet the Korean people will be remembered by all who came to their country for their courtesy and helpfulness, their eagerness to please. They made a distinctive contribution to the Olympic Movement, and to the world beyond that.

HARMONY

AND

PROGRESS

OPENING HAND

SWEET DAY

Opening Ceremonies so often disclose the soul of the nation, and so it was with the Republic of Korea. As they opened their arms to one hundred and fifty nine other nations, and five billion television viewers, we saw the people for what they are: tranquil yet with an inner strength, graceful yet energetic, moulded by ancient dynasties yet ambitiously modern.

The Republic of Korea is dramatically successful, but the Opening Ceremony of Seoul gave us not assertiveness or aggression but gentleness. The people are strong and determined: their pageant was a picture of history, color and elegance. For three hours, on a morning when the Gods graced Seoul with sun and an autumn-blue sky, the emphasis was not on achievement, which is as much a part of the Korean story as it is of the Olympic Games, but on harmony and friendship.

As Seoul opened an Olympic Games with a ceremony that was a triumphal celebration of contemporary international recognition for the nation, they simultaneously captured that mystic, indefinable quality that is the quintessence of Olympism.

The occasion gave the watching world that sense of joy that is experienced mostly with small children and the spontaneity of their smiles. There was about this day a sweetness, at times almost a deliberate naivety, that was enchantingly oriental. So appropriate, the involvement of thousands of children in the Ceremony epitomized a basic premise of the Olympic Games: that our future lies with youth.

It was thoughtful of the organizing committee to reward thousands of those unable to be inside the stadium with the spectacle of the Han River Boat Parade. Inside, the ceremony Greeting the Sun began the morning with primeval dignity synonymous with the origins of the Olympic concept itself. The procession of the massive Dragon Drum; the unification of Heaven, Earth and Man enacted by ethereal maidens; the Light of Genesis symbolizing creation, with 1,600 modern dancers: here was an expression of mankind devoid of all conventional materialist trappings.

Thus we moved towards the formal ceremonies of flag and flame and oath. The national president arrives. Oriental ladies in the presidential box discreetly shade their pale complexions from the sun's rays behind fans, while for an hour the teams march into the stadium.

CEREMONY IN HAND

SMILES OF EXPECTATION

The Netherlands wave their orange umbrella shooting-sticks upon which they will wisely later be able to rest. Japan wave Rose of Sharon bouquets, the Korean national flower, Canada throw frisbees into the crowd and everybody throws smiles of expectation.

Now Park Seh-jik and Juan Antonio Samaranch, respective presidents of the organizing committee and the International Olympic Committee, give their greetings, and President Roh Tae-woo declares the Games open.

As the flag arrives, jet airplanes weave five rings in the clear sky. Into the stadium comes the flame, at the climax of a journey through Korea that has brought emotional involvement for many in countless villages, now borne along by a national hero: Sohn Kee-chung, 76-year-old winner of the marathon as an ersatz Japanese in 1936.

SYMBOL OF HOPE

The benign champion skips like a six-year-old through the crowd of athletes pressing on to the track around him, and the flame is passed to Lim Chun-ae, unheralded winner of three gold medals at the Asian Games of 1986. Three cauldron-lighters then rise towards the roof of the stadium in one of the few moments of mechanization: and the symbol of hope is alight. In a moment of magical timing, five jets simultaneously leave a plume of colored trailers just above the stadium roof-top, and seventy six parachutists come plummeting into the arena like messengers from Zeus.

Now follows a kaleidoscope of Korean color and youth: the Hwakwan Dance of the Yi Dynasty, a masked dance of Chaos, and the restoration or order and discipline by a Taekwondo team of one thousand. Then, in a minute of deep silence, into the stadium, bowling his hoop, runs Yun Tae-ung, born on day Seoul was granted the Games in 1981. Bewitching young children follow, with careless play, and finally the classic Gonori folk-game of contesting dragons: the harmony of Yin and Yang in Korean philosophy, with traditional reconciliation.

It is, too, the ultimate symbolism of the Games of re-unification.

As Park Seh-jik has said in his speech to an audience in 115 countries: "The land of the Morning Calm is about to become the arena for the dreams and ideals of young men and women from around the world." We who are watching dream with them, and there are some moist eyes as we depart for the commencement of 16 days perhaps unique even in the history of the Olympic Games.

The Dragon Drum procession, a tradition of the Yi Dynasty preceded and introduced the Dynasty's kings. The accompanying music consists of four parts: the drumbeat, the symbol of Korea, a section to greet the world, the drum procession, and welcoming cheers.
Sixteen hundred modern dancers spin in center stadium, forming the light of creation and extending their 'welcome' to the world audience.
The entry of the President of the Republic of Korea and the First Lady.

아르헨티나
ARGENTINA

42

One of many mass game formations, this one symbolizing the Seoul Olympic emblem is followed by the entry of athletes. Then Park Seh-jik, President of the Seoul Olympic Organizing Committee moves to center stage to deliver his speech and introduce Juan Antonio Samaranch, President of the International Olympic Committee who gives his welcoming address.

These pigeons take a break following their release as part of the twenty four hundred set free to symbolize freedom and peace.

Eight Korean gold medalists in previous Olympic Games enter the stadium holding the Olympic flag.
Part of the Han River boat parade, just prior to the opening ceremony, symbolizing the opening of the city of Seoul to the Olympic Games.

The lighting of the Seoul Olympic Flame announces the opening of the Games of the 24th Olympiad. Sohn Kee-chung, passes the flame to Lim Chun-ae who provides it to the cauldron-lighters. As the flame begins to blaze, the Olympic Rings are formed by jets and parachutists descend into the stadium.

A delightful potpourri of events followed the official opening of the Games to symbolize both the meaning of humanity and the spirit of the Seoul Olympics. Highlights included the Flower Crown Dance, over 1,000 members of a taekwondo team, Yun Tae-ung rolling a hoop and Gonori, the game to symbolize the harmony and unity of everything that is opposite.

The Kangbok, prayer of blessings, Chail Dance and Hwakwan Dance, a celebration of peace are performed to the delight of young and old. Whenever Koreans hold a festival they set up awnings and hold a banquet. The Chail Dance utilized wrapping cloth as a instrument of dance, expressing the festivity of the flickering awnings. The Hwakwan Dance represented the peaceful times of yesterear when heaven was in harmany with the earth. Drums, balloons and smiles were found everywhere.

DAY1

A small Korean woman, Choo Nan-yool, sits on a stool with an expression of intense concentration. The clean line of her jaw is set firm, her eyes are fixed, gazing ahead in private thought. In this moment she represents not merely herself but her country. At stake is the first gold medal of the Olympic Games of 1988, never mind that it is in the demonstration sport of Taekwondo, and therefore listed unofficially. On the other side of the mat is Maria Angela Naranjo of Spain: and seated in the front row of the gallery is Juan Antonio Samaranch, Spanish president of the IOC, who will be presenting the medals. For Choo it is probably the sporting moment of her life-time.

She is 16, and only started the sport four years ago, and it is only this year that she has gained selection for the national team. She is a student at Pusan, enjoys music, and would like one day to be a professor. But now: now she must bring all her skill to bear to beat the taller blond girl facing her. They bow to the audience, and to each other. The crowd stamps its feet. The bout is on.

4

1. *Arlene Limas of the United States gets the gold and gets emotional in the women's welterweight final.*
2. *Chung Kook-hyun, welterweight winner, spins to deliver a blow with the right foot.*
3. *The Taekwondo Stadium, one of Seoul's profusion of modern venues.*
4. *Competition breeds mutual appreciation.*

1. Choo Nan-yool, Korean winner of the women's taekwondo, the demonstration sport, flyweight class, takes the initiative.
2. The face of Korean youth. A child taekwondo demonstrator.
3. Ha Tae-kyung, Korean gold medalist in men's flyweight, gets on top.

4. Your move. Chung Kook-hyun, Korean winner, and runner-up Luigi D'Oriano of Italy, spar together.
5. Anyone's match, it seems, in a welterweight bout.

3

4

1

Naranjo, a handsome woman, has her feet heavily strapped for protection from further injury. Soon, however, it is evident that the Korean is the faster, spinning to deliver high blows with the feet on the jacket target area. Naranjo is outmaneuvered and uncertain.

At the end of the three rounds there can be no doubt who is the winner. Choo has been on the attack throughout, struck all the decisive blows. As the end of the contest is sounded, she buries her face in her hands and is embraced by her coach. They must wait a few moments, but the judges' decision can be only a formality.

The ceremonious red carpet is rolled out, a pageant to be performed many times in the coming two weeks. This occasion belongs to Choo, and to Naranjo, the silver medalist, and to Pai Yun-yao of Taipeh and Mayumi Pejo of the United States, the bronze medalist. There is no prouder person in Seoul than Choo as Samaranch steps forward to hang around her neck the medal that has no price.

It proves to be a successful opening evening for Korea in its national sport. In the men's fly-weight, the gold medal goes to Ha Tae-kyung, and so too in the men's welter-weight, to Chung Kook-hyun. In the women's welter-weight, Kim Ji-sook can manage only the silver, defeated by Arlene Limas of the United States. The Koreans this night have held their heads high.

5   2

At volleyball it has not been such a good story for the hosts, defeated in their opening match at Hanyang University in a stunning reversal. The Korean men's team won the first two sets against Sweden 15-10 and 15-5, and confidently pressed in what seemed likely to be a final third set to lead 5-0, only to lose their command. Sweden took the set 15-12. When the hosts led 14-12 in the fourth, it again seemed that victory was theirs, but the chance slid away, Sweden taking the set 17-15. In the final set, Korea slumped to lose 15-4.

The Netherlands, with only one player under 6 ft.-5 in. tall, had become dark-horse candidates leading up to the Games, and in the opening match they defeated the small but quick French team in four sets.

1. Gustafson of Sweden attacking Korea at the net.
2. Korea defends.
3. Let's dance, say Chang and Lee of Korea.
4. You don't get by! A Frenchman defends the net against Netherlands.

8

5. Stop that one. Sweden about to strike against Korea.
6. Four-in-a line defence. Tholse and Bjorne of Sweden raise blockade.
7. Sweden look badly positioned with Korea about to strike.
8. Go! Go! Sweden!

5

4

At the start of the football tournament, the Federal Republic of Germany established itself as a favorite with a convincing 3-0 win over China, including two goals from Mill, in the match in Pusan. In the south-west city of Kwangju, Italy overran Guatemala, brought into the finals as a substitute for Mexico, which had been banned from international tournaments.

1. *Goertz of the Federal Republic of Germany putting on the style against China.*
2. *Let's make this colorful.*
3. *What was it my Chinese coach was saying?*
4. *Anyone's ball: Federal Republic of Germany against China.*
5. *Try, try and try again.*

1. They shall not pass: French volleyball defenders.
2. They have to look after their knees in this game.
3. Meet me afterwards for lunch at 2 pm, suggests Jurkowitz of France.
4. Many more bandages and this Korean player will look like a mummy.
5. France concentrate on the net.

2

2

3

4

1. Well, this is it. Here we go.
2. Xu Yanmei, one of China's squad of supreme divers, gold medalist in women's 10 meter platform event.
3. Michele Mitchell of the United States, the silver medalist, in a world of her own.

3

DAY2

2

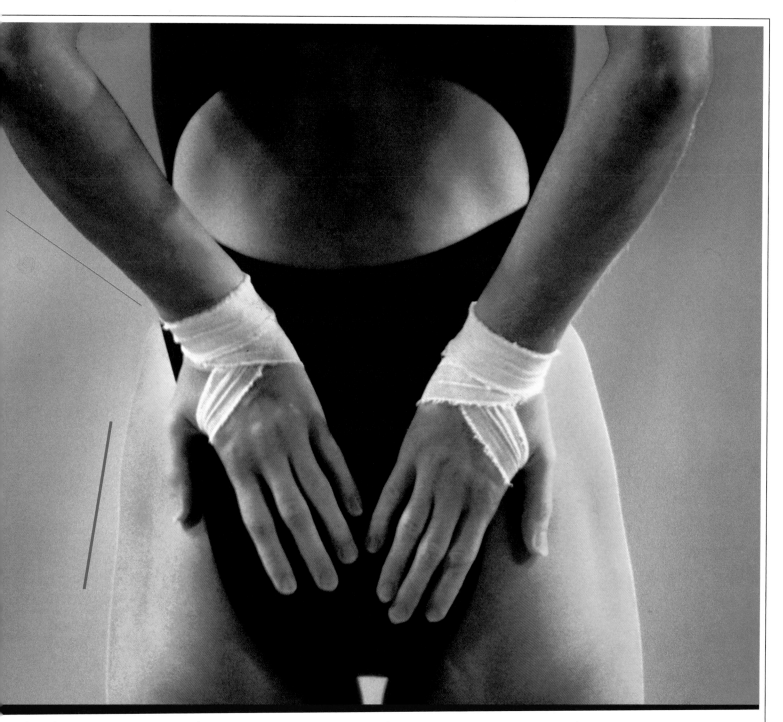

WHAT DO THE CHINESE WANT?

The question with the Chinese is less a matter of what do they do well than what do they want to do well. With the size of their population, it is a matter of

deciding on what to concentrate. Diving is a case in point. With a natural acrobatic agility — witnessed in perfection in their National Games acrobatics event — they first turned to gymnastics, then to diving. Such sports lend themselves to Confucian discipline. In the women's platform 10 meter event, the gold medal went to the 17-year-old Xu Yanmei, a secondary school student from Beijing.

With her body curled in mid air, her head tucked against her knees, Xu has momentarily a sculptured, almost fetal stillness. She won by just over eight points from Michele Mitchell of Florida, also the silver medalists at Los Angeles in 1984. Wendy Williams of the USA took the bronze.

HUGE APPLAUSE

Much was expected of the other Chinese entry, Chen Xiaodan, a rising young star of only fourteen. She led on the first-day preliminaries, with Xu lying third behind Mitchell, who is now 27. Chen, always pushing her technique to the extreme, received huge applause from the 7,000 spectators at the Chamshil pool for her seventh dive on the first day: a one-and-a-half somersault with three-and-a-half twist.

But on the second day Chen was inconsistent, quite the reverse of Xu. Chen attempted dives that were increasingly difficult, made regular errors, and finished only

fifth behind another 14-year-old, Elena Miroshina of the Soviet Union. Some sports really are becoming the Schoolgirl Games. Xu's steadiness won her the gold, though Mitchell, attempting slightly less elaborate dives, maintained her second place through experience. Williams, with the second best marks on the final dive, moved ahead of Anjela Stassioulevitch from fourth place to snatch the bronze.

SO LATE

The story of the first Gold medal of the Games, in women's air rifle, was the failure of the favorite, Vessela Letcheva of Bulgaria, the world champion. She failed even to make the final eight. The winner was Irina Chilova, a Soviet sports instructor and mother of an eight-year-old daughter, whose name was not even included on the official Soviet team handbook, so late was the decision to select her. The judgement of the Soviet selectors, in all sports, is a regular lesson to other nations. Chilova beat Silvia Sperber of the Federal Republic of Germany by one point, on 498.5, and was three points clear of her compatriot Anna Maloukhina. Another favorite fell on the first day at the Taenung Shooting Range, when Igor Bassinski, the Soviet world champion, could finish only third in the men's free pistol. Sorin Babii of Romania took the gold with 660 points, three ahead of Ragnar Skanaker of Sweden, who beat Bassinski in a shoot-out for the silver.

1. Profile of concentration in the 10 meters pistol event.
2. Andreas Wecker of the GDR demonstrates parallel bars technique.
3. Dmitri Bilozerchev of the Soviet Union on bars: a remarkable recovery following severe injury.
4. Xu Zhiqiang of China a fraction off balance.
5. Brad Peter (Canada) swallow dives on the vault.
6. Terry Bartlett of Britain raises a puff of resin dust on the vaulting horse.
7. A Canadian with his legs slightly off line.

1

6

5

7

DRAMATIC START

The host country's first medal of the Games — demonstration Taekwondo medals on Saturday excepted — came when Chun Byung-kwan took the silver in the Weightlifting 52 kilogram class (114⅔ lbs), in which Sevdalin Marinov of Bulgaria set a new world record of 270.0 kg (595¼ lbs). There was a dramatic start to the men's hockey when the Korean team, the Asian Games champions, came from two goals behind to draw with Great Britain, one of the favorites.

Trust the German Democratic Republic to come up with something new. Their four-man cycling team won the 100 kilometer road race time trial at a remarkable 50.935 kph average (31.651 MPH), with special reduced-friction frames. The argument grows for standardized, one-class equipment.

1

1. *Sevdalin Marinov of Bulgaria, winner of the 52 kg (114⅔ lbs.) title. It's ... nearly ... there.*

1. Solid support among the GDR in the 100 kilometer time trial.
2. The USA gets its head down in the 100 km time trial.
3. A Korean player has his knuckles painfully rapped against Britain.
4. Break for talks: Australia versus Kenya.
5. Britain celebrate one of their two goals in the 2-2 draw with Korea.
6. Missed it. A Canadian on the slide against FRG.
7. Someone wants to discuss a good tactical idea for Spain against Pakistan.

1. Sven Tippelt of the GDR is airborne, almost.
2. Levitation by Li Chunyang of China.
3. A Chinese gymnast defies gravity on the rings.

THE GOLD FOR ARMSTRONG

For Duncan Armstrong, September 16 and 19 could both prove to be particularly important days in his life. The day before the opening of the Games, FINA, the International Amateur Swimming Federation, decided that swimmers might now be permitted to earn money from endorsements and sponsorship. On the third day of the Games, Armstrong achieved one of the most startling upsets in the history of the sport, when he won the men's 200 meters freestyle in world record time.

Certainly the joy of this 20-year-old Australian will, in his moment of triumph, have excluded any thought of material reward. An Olympic crown is without valuation. But victory will have done him no financial harm. Swimming has finally moved the way of other newly professional sports.

Victory was remarkable when you consider whom Armstrong beat: Michael Gross, the defending champion and previous record holder from the Federal Republic of Germany, who could finish no half a second behind Armstrong's new best time of 1 min. 47.25 secs.

PRIVATE DUEL

Gross and Biondi had been expected to fight a private duel for the gold, and there had been speculation about Biondi emulating Mark Spitz's seven golds in Munich: speculation which he had been quick to dismiss, on the grounds of modern specialization. "I'm convinced that will never happen again" Biondi had said. Well, certainly not this time. Gross was first into the water. Illegally. His false start was the only time he was in the lead. Armstrong, who is better known back home as a 400 meters swimmer, was in Biondi's wake until after the final turn, a tactical plan established beforehand with Laurie Lawrence, his coach. "I ran him down" Armstrong said afterwards, with pardonable exaggeration. "I jumped into the trough (Biondi's) and just body surfed in!".

1

2

better than fifth, and Matt Biondi, the record holder for 100 metres freestyle, who took the bronze medal. Anders Holmertz of Sweden gained the silver, just over

1. *Adrian Moorhouse of Britain, disqualified in 1984, finds fulfillment in winning the 100 meters breaststroke.*
2. *A major surprise as Duncan Armstrong of Australia beats the favorites Gross and Biondi in the 200 meters freestyle.*

DAY**3**

BUSH HAT

Biondi was gracious in defeat; and, surprisingly, pleased. "The 200 is my worst event, the one I have the least natural talent for, and I won a medal" he said. Lawrence, extrovert in Hawaiian shirt and Australian bush hat, was exultant. "We know Duncan's not as talented as the others" he said, "but he's been working for two years, building up his speed. What he used was guts and conditioning."

Janet Evans from California, the first woman since Kornelia Ender of the GDR to hold three world records simultaneously — 400, 800 and 1,500 meters freestyle — was widely predicted to win the 400 meters individual medley: and did so.

The 17-year-old American is of unconventional build for a champion swimmer: a mere 5 ft.6 in and 101 lbs (1.66 m, 46 kg). She has been swimming almost before she could walk, and is exceptional not only for her small stature but her absence of style. Her strength would seem to be in her mind; though she would not be seen at her very best in the Games because the 1,500 m, in which she is the first woman to break 16 minutes, was not on the schedule. Her medley time of 4 min. 37.76 secs. was the third fastest ever swum, an American record, and gave her a comfortable victory over Neomi Lung of Romania and Daniela Hunger of GDR.

1. Janet Evans (US) seems to be running rather than swimming when winning the 400 individual medley.
2. A smile tells all. Janet Evans wins the 400.
3. A moment of serious reflection during the national anthem.

ULTIMATE COMPENSATION

Kristin Otto, renowned champion of the GDR, led from start to finish to win the women's 100 meters in 54.93 secs., just over a tenth of a second outside the Olympic record of Barbara Krause, set in 1980 in Moscow. Zhuang Yong of China, fifth at the turn, beat Catherine Plewinski of France by two hundredths of a second to take the silver medal.

Adrian Moorhouse of Britain, disqualified in Los Angeles for an illegal turn, earned the ultimate compensation when he won the men's 100 meters breaststroke. He did so by only one hundredth of a second, a refinement of technology which left Karoly Guttler of Hungary with the silver medal. The disappointment of 1984 caused Moorhouse to retire for a while, and how he must now welcome the decision to have made another attempt. It was not looking promising at the turn, at which Dmitri Volkow of the Soviet Union was ahead, but Moorhouse and Guttler steadily overhauled him. Moorhouse's childhood coach was there at the Olympic Park to see it happen, only because he won a free trip to Seoul in a Hong Kong newspaper competition.

1

2

1. Hunger of the GDR is relaxed for the start.
2. See, I can touch my toes.
3. More ways than one of entering the water.
4. Arm aloft from Kristin Otto of the GDR signals 100 meters freestyle victory, one of an armful.

1. *Somebody get me out of here quick. Chi Wang of Chinese Taipei.*

2. *Miroslav Varga Of Czechoslovakia is congratulated by fellow medalists after winning the small-bore prone.*

THING OF THE PAST

Such lack of funds among swimmers and coaches may now be a thing of the past, with the change in rule by FINA. Swimming may still not be a full-time occupation, but appearance money as well as endorsements are to be allowed so long as they are paid into trust funds. FINA will no longer use the word 'amateur' other than, illogically, in its official name.

There was general dissatisfaction throughout the Olympic Village with the decision to disqualify Anthony Hembrick, an American middleweight boxer, when he failed to arrive on time for his bout with the Korean Ha Jong-ho. There were jeers even from home crowd followers when Ha stood in an empty ring and was given a walk-over after three minutes.

U.S. boxing officials lodged an official protest against the decision, on the basis that the boxer had been unable to get on a bus from the Village because it was full and there had not been another for half an hour. The Tunisian chairman of the appeals commission rejected Hembrick's case on a casting vote. The whole episode seemed out of character with the intended spirit of the Games. But Hembrick should have left earlier.

2

UNCOMMON COURAGE

There are champions...and there are heroes. Greg Louganis revealed the qualities of both when he retained his springboard diving title with a combination of unrivalled skill and uncommon courage.

In winning his third Olympic gold medal, he not only recovered after hitting his head on the board during the preliminaries, qualifying for the finals after having four stitches in his lacerated scalp, but had the nerve and the concentration to repeat the same highly technical dive the following day.

Words fail most of us in moments of stress, and it is not surprising that athletes and coaches are given to cliches. Yet the U.S. team manager reflected everyone's admiration when she said: "Louganis showed us that he is made of granite."

4

1

DAY 4

3

2

FAST SPINNERS

Although the 28-year-old Louganis is synonymous with grace, he was already under enough pressure from the improving Chinese without the misfortune that befell him. Before the competition he had said: "People say I seem calm, but I'm human, I'm insecure about the way I perform. The Chinese are spectacular, they spin fast. That's something I would like to emulate."

On the first day, Louganis was leading Tan Liangde, the silver medalist in Los Angeles, who had twice beaten him in 1988. On the ninth dive, Louganis's head struck the board during a reverse two-and-a-half somersault in the pike position. He made a bad entry, and though he was able to pull himself out of the pool unaided, low points dropped him from first to fifth.

When he re-appeared 30 minutes later, his head stitched, the crowd applauded. He smiled in appreciation. His next dive, a reverse one-and-a-half somersault with three-and-a-half twists, was the second hardest he performs. A perfect execution, with a composure that was hard to comprehend under the circumstances, revived his fortunes.

HARDLY A RIPPLE

On the second day, there was no reprieve in the intensity of the rivalry, for Tan Liangde and Li Deliang were at the heels of Louganis all the way. Yet he continued to perform as one of the greatest of champions. His entries were clean, with hardly a ripple. His smiles were modest compared to his brilliance.

Early that morning, to erase any abrasions that might still linger on his confidence, Louganis had been through his entire program in a 40-minute work-out. By the time he came to compete, his spirits were as crisp as a newly laundered shirt. It was not until the ninth dive that the gold medal was assured. Tan Liangde could have overtaken him at any stage. Yet from his opening dive, receiving a row of 9.0 s from the judges, his confidence was secure. Though Tan Liangde led after the fourth round, Louganis immediately went ahead again on the fifth dive. How would he be on the repeat of his critical ninth dive?

1. Greg Louganis, surviving a split head, is relieved to win the springboard title again.
2. Tan Liangde of China pressed Louganis all the way in men's springboard.
3. A sculptor's perfect model.
4. Hesitation before the leap into action.

2

1. *Tsai Wen-yee of Chinese Taipei finds no comfort in taking a rest on his weights.*
2. *Naim Suleymanoglu, a former Bulgarian now representing Turkey, takes the strain in winning the 60 kg weightlifting class.*

TENSE FINAL DIVE

"I was nervous, because of what happened the day before," he admitted afterwards. "I knew everybody was watching closely, that I just had to remember I'd done it so many times before." It was, in the event, adequate. Tan Liangde would have to settle for the silver. Li Deliang, in a tense final dive, took the bronze only four points ahead of Albin Killat of FRG. Elsewhere, Naim Suleymanoglu of Turkey gave his new country its first Olympic gold medal in 20 years in weightlifting in the 60 kg (132¼ lbs) class, setting world records all along the way. He improved his own records in the snatch with lifts of 150.5 kg (331¾ lbs) and 152 kg (335 lbs), and then lifted 188.5 kg (415½ lbs) and 190 kg (419 lbs) in the clean and jerk. His combined total was 342.5 kg (755 lbs), which was 7.5 kg (16½ lbs) more than his former record set in 1986.

The Soviet Union expectedly won the men's team gymnastics title, by a clear margin from the GDR, with Japan taking the bronze medal. Dmitry Monakov continued the Soviet haul of medals when he won the clay trap shooting in a sudden death shoot-out. The 1987 world champion, Monakov won the title after tying with Miloslav Bednarik of Czechoslovakia on 222 points in the six-man final at the Taenung Range. Bednarik, who lost his world title to Monakov last year, conceded the gold when he missed his eight sudden death target. Frans Peeters of Belgium won the bronze from Francisco Boza of Peru and Bean van Limbeek of Netherlands in a shoot-off, following a three-way tie on 219 points. "This sport is all a question of nerves" Monakov said afterwards. Who would have guessed?

IN TEARS

Goran Maksimovic won Yugoslavia's first gold medal of the Games when he took the men's air rifle competition with a total of 695.6 points. Nicolas Berthelot of France and Johann Riederer of FRG were respectively second and third. The first eight all broke the Olympic record. Oliver Gasper, a 15-year-old Hungarian, was in tears when eliminated from the final eight qualifiers because An Byung-kyun, a Korean on the same score, had the better last round.

In taekwondo, the demonstration martial arts sport, Korean men and women won nine of the 16 medals, followed by the United States, Chinese Taipei and Denmark.

There was depression for Nigeria, runners-up in the 1988 African Football Championship, when they lost 3-1 to Yugoslavia, following their 4-0 rout by Brazil on Sunday. This left them bottom of their group. The host nation, hoping to qualify for the quarter-finals, were disappointingly held to a draw by the United States. The Soviet Union, tournament favorites but held to a draw by Korea in their opening match, moved to the head of their group with a 2-1 win over Argentina.

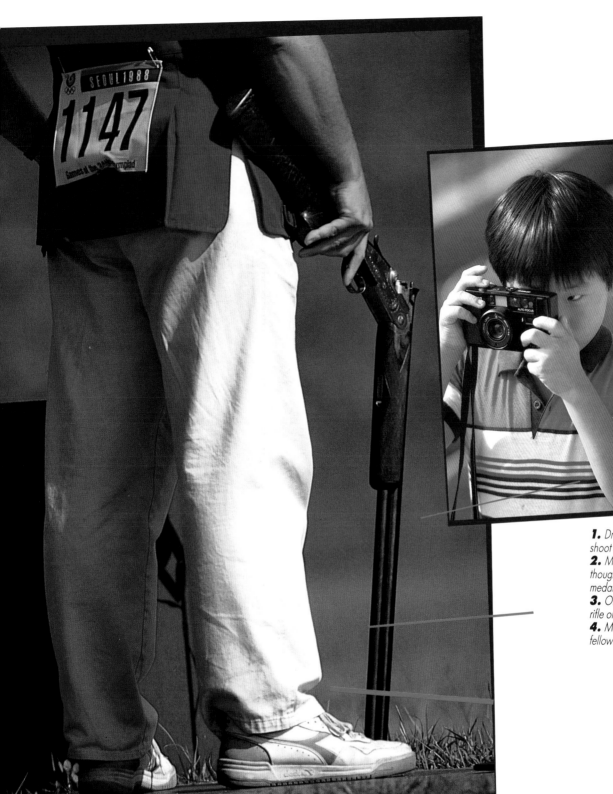

1. *Dmitri Monakov waiting for the bird; trap shoot champion.*
2. *Miloslav Bednarik has had enough; though he did win the trap shoot silver medal.*
3. *Off duty moment. Daniele Cioni rests rifle on toe.*
4. *Maksimovic of Yugoslavia (centre) and fellow medalists celebrate rifle presentation.*

3

1. *Don't look now, but I think we're being watched.*

2. *Atanas Komchev of Bulgaria receives a friendly hug in victory from his coach.*

3. *Koskela of Finland does not look optimistic against Komchev, and must accept the silver medal.*

4. *I can't hear his heart beat, but he seems alive enough.*

1. Multi-medalist Matt Biondi takes a breather.
2. Anthony Nesty, the first black Olympic swimming champion, first ever medalist of Suriname, acknowledges acclaim for 100 meters butterfly victory.
3. Biondi finishes the 4 x 100 relay to colleagues' acclaim.
4. We did it. USA rejoice over 4 x 200 medley relay victory.
5. Mid-race for American 4 x 200 relay team.

DAY**5**

3

4

It is the small countries, marching into the stadium among the grand and famous, who give the Olympic Games their unique sporting ambience. The big and the strong mostly win the medals. When they do not, we all tend to cheer a little louder. That was the way it was at the swimming pool when a gold and a silver medal went to little known competitors from tiny nations. On a day when three world records were broken in other races, the acclaim was for Anthony Nesty of Surinam and Silvia Poll of Costa Rica.

There is only one pool in the whole of Surinam, the former Dutch colony in Latin America. In defeating Matt Biondi, the famed American, by the smallest possible margin of one hundredth of a second, Nesty set four records: he became the first black swimming champion of the Olympic Games, the first South American Swimming Champion, the first medalist of his country and, for good measure, he set a new Olympic record for the 100 meters butterfly. He was Suriname's only competitor in the Games.

5

1

2

3

1. *A deep breath before the start for Michael Gross.*
2. *A wave from Silke Hoerner of the GDR.*
3. *Stewards line up for instruction.*
4. *Hoerner sits up between strokes in the 200 meters breaststroke, such is her thrust.*
5. *Tamas Darnyi of Hungary, 400 meter individual medley champion.*

HALF A SECOND DOWN

Nesty was born in Trinidad, and moved to Suriname when he was five months old, and began swimming when he was five. There are fewer than 1000 swimmers in the country's one 50-meter pool and 10 others of 25 meters; though Nesty had already come to hold four South American records. He was the 1987 Pan-American champion, so the pedigree was there, but the final had been expected to be between Biondi, Michael Gross of the Federal Republic of Germany and Andy Jameson of Britain, the fastest qualifier. At the turn, Nesty was half a second down, but caught Biondi in the last meter, when the American coasted on his final stroke. Jameson was third.

The triumph of Poll in the women's 200 meters freestyle was almost equally unique. Her silver medal was the first won in any sport by Costa Rica, and the first by a woman swimmer from Central or Latin America. Heike Friedrich of the German Democratic Republic, the world record holder, set an Olympic record of 1 min. 57.65 secs., a second ahead of Poll, who was two tenths of a second ahead of Manuella Stellmach of the GDR.

4

5

1, 2. Guenchev of Bulgaria lifts for gold in 67.5 kg (148¾ lbs.) class, then his celebration which was short lired guencher was disqualified and stripped of the gold after testing positive for steroids. Another warning for future Olympians.

3. Kim Young-han has a decided edge on Jean Manga of Canada.

4. Korean girl, cool drink.

5. It is not every week an Olympic Games passes through your country.

6. Bravo! Ole! Hurrah!

7. For two weeks, Seoul was the city of friendliness.

There was pride, too, for the host nation when Kim Young-nam won its first gold medal, coming from behind against Daoulet Tourlykhanov of the Soviet Union in the 74 kg (163 lbs). Greco-Roman wrestling. Thus he continued a Korean Republic trend, for it was in this sport that their first ever gold medal was won, in 1976, and their first in the Games of 1984.

5

1   7   2

6

3

4

PERSUADE TO CONTINUE

In Los Angeles, Kim had finished fourth, and almost decided to retire from the sport, but was persuaded to continue by the inspiration of Kim Weon-kee, who had won the gold medal in the 60 kg (132¼ lbs). class.

When Kim went behind in the first half of·the bout, his wife Ra Hyang, who was in the crowd, was in tears. When he won, students of Hampyong Agricultural High School, his former college, who were watching on television, spent the rest of the night in celebration. There was further satisfaction for the hosts when their women's hockey team recorded a startling 4-1 victory over the Federal Republic of Germany, the Olympic and World Cup silver medalists. Lim Kye-sook, on the right wing, scored twice for the winners.

1. Seoul was a city in which to try new tastes — if you could manage the chopsticks.
2. I've got pins from just everywhere.
3. The Games are all about meeting old friends and meeting new ones.
4. Have a nice day.
5. Chelle Stack of America reveals a flexible backbone on the beam.
6. Jasna Sekaric of Yugoslavia lines up winning pistol shot.

3

4

1

2

5

6

1. Taking aim, Air Pistol competition.
2. Are they lending the cheers?

1

2

1. A slight case of miscalculation between Green of Australia and his horse.
2. More bad luck for Australia. Keach and mount take an unscheduled drink.
3. All day long, unending opponents, mounting fatigue: the Modern Pentathlon event.
4. The greatest all-rounders of the Games. Hungary, Italy (right) and Britain take the Modern Pentathlon medals after five days of riding, fencing, swimming, shooting and running.
5. A perfect pair. Mark Todd of New Zealand and the immaculate Charisma repeat their equestrian three-day event individual gold.
6. Matheas Baumann, of the Federal Republic of Germany, and Shamrock keep a sharp eye on the fence.

3

4

5

2

ELATION, FULFILLMENT AND DIGNITY

If the Olympic Games are still about sportsmanship as much as about sport, then the modern pentathlon and equestrian three-day event lie at the heart of things. In no other sports is there to be found more graciousness in defeat or modesty in victory.

In the space of six hours there were equal scenes of elation, fulfillment and dignity, first at Olympic Park, then at Kwachon Equestrian Center. Janos Martinek of Hungary in the pentathlon and Mark Todd of New Zealand in the three-day event were individual winners instantly acclaimed by their rivals. Both sports are threatened in the long-term by the cost factor, measured against the relatively small number of participating nations around the world. Yet Baron de Coubertin believed them to be sports which personified the character of the Games. As Todd, who received his medal from The Princess Royal, president of the equestrian federation, said afterwards: "Equestrianism belongs to the Games".

Martinek, at 23 the youngest ever to win the title, ran the race of his life in the cross-country, the fifth and final event of the sport. With a 29-point deficit on Vakhtang Iagorachvili of the Soviet Union, the leader after four days, Martinek had a ten second gap to close over the 4,000 meters course. With the sixth fastest time of the 63 runners, 13 mins. 3.19 secs., the exhausted Martinek had handsomely overhauled Iagorachvili by the finishing line, with an 18 seconds margin over the tough, hilly course. The Russian was also overtaken by Carlo Massullo of Italy, who took the silver medal after closing a 29 seconds handicap to finish half a minute ahead.

Hungary won the team gold, the second time they had gained the double, previously achieved only by Italy in 1984 and Hungary in 1960.

In a tense battle for the bronze, Great Britain, having begun the day in fifth place behind the Soviet Union and France, just got home by a collective eight points, or a fraction under three seconds: a whisker of a margin at the end of five gruelling days. They had to wait more than half an hour for the judges' decision.

For Todd, it was also a double of rare distinction. Defending the title he won in Los Angeles, and riding the same supreme horse, Charisma, he had had a clear round on the second day in the cross-country event. Going into the show-jumping, he held off the challenge of Ian Stark and Virginia Leng, both of Britain, conceding only five penalty points with one fence dislodged.

Only Charles Pahud of the Netherlands, in 1928/1932, had previously achieved the double. Todd will now retire Charisma, and look for another horse. The Federal Republic of Germany, bronze medalist in Los Angeles, won the team gold.

1

1. *Winning gold medals seems no effort to Kristin Otto of the German Democratic Republic.*
2. *It's that irrepressible Biondi again.*
3. *A slim-line Janet Evans sets off for gold with a deep breath in the 400 meters freestyle.*
4. *Igor Polyanski of the Soviet Union is first away and wins the 200 meters backstroke.*

THE FIRST TRIPLE GOLD MEDALIST

At the Olympic Park swimming pool, Kristin Otto of the GDR became the first triple gold medalist of the Games in Seoul, while the Americans Matt Biondi and Janet Evans won their second gold. Otto, aged 22, who earlier had won the 100 meters freestyle, now captured the 100 meters backstroke and 400 meters freestyle relay.

The exceptional 17-year-old Evans set a world record of 4 mins. 3.85 secs. improving her own previous record, in winning the 400 meters freestyle. Biondi set a new Olympic record, in winning the 100 meters freestyle in 48.63 secs. The only other gold medal of the day was won by Igor Polianski of the Soviet Union in the men's 200 meters backstroke.

1

2

3

4

100

VLADIMIR ARTEMOV NEAR PERFECTION

The Soviet Union having earlier won the men's team gymnastics title, there was a surprise in the all-round individual event when Vladimir Artemov won the gold medal with a display of near perfection. Dmitri Bilozertchev, aged 21, had recovered miraculously from a car accident three years ago which shattered his left leg. Fighting his way back into the team, he had regained his pre-eminent position in the sport, and during three days of competition in Seoul he recorded six perfect scores. Wretchedly for him, one serious error on the second day left him with the bronze: small consolation for a genius of this sport who twice won the world championship. Another compatriot, Valeri Lioukine, took the silver.

1. Cynthia Cooper looks for an opening.
2. A study in perfection from Vladimir Artemov, gold medalist.
3. Another Soviet clean sweep. Artemov and colleagues face the cameras.
4. Olga Strajeva of the Soviet Union comes to grief in the gymnastics team final.
5. She's trying to tell someone something.
6. Choi beats his man. Republic of Korea versus Argentina.

1. *Fichtel asks for an explanation … and gets thrown in the air.*
2. *Sport, not war. An ancient, elegant form of aggression.*
3. *Rival team-mates Fichtel and Bau, FRG, congratulate each other on gold and silver in foil.*
4. *Mette Jacobsen of Denmark on guard.*

MORE FAIR-PLAY PLEASE

The sixth day of the Games was marred by an incident in boxing. Keith Walker, a New Zealand referee, was jostled in the ring by Korean Republic officials following a disputed decision in which Alexandar Hristov of Bulgaria was given a points verdict over Byun Jong-Il, a local bantamweight (54 kg) (119 lbs). The fight itself had been controversial, and, when a 4-1 verdict was given to the Bulgarian, several Korean officials entered the ring in protest. For some while Byun Jong-Il refused to leave the ring.

The international Amateur Boxing Association subsequently announced that five Korean officials, including Lee Hong-Soo, the chief trainer, were indefinitely suspended.

The IOC Medical Commission announced that positive tests had been recorded against Mitko Grablev of Bulgaria, winner of the 56 kg (123½ lbs), weightlifting event, for furosemide, a banned diuretic; and against Alex Watson, the Australian pentathlete, for excessive caffeine.

1. *A study of the marathon runner's mental isolation. Rosa Mota in her private world.*
2. *Rosa Mota of Portugal looks pained in the morning sunlight, but she was too fast for everyone in the marathon.*
3. *Randy Barnes of America winds up for second place.*
4. *Have I really done it? Ulf Timmermann of the GDR wins the shot put gold medal.*
5. *The hard way to see Seoul. Rosa Mota leads the sight-seeing.*

FOUR HEROINES?

There were three heroines this day, though Romania might claim there was a fourth. On the opening day of the athletics program, Rosa Mota, the darling of Portugal, repeated her triumph of 1987 in the world championships by winning the women's marathon. Kristin Otto of the GDR became the first quadruple gold medalist of these Games by taking the women's 100 meters butterfly with an Olympic record. And Elena Chouchounova of the Soviet Union claimed the much prized individual all-round award in women's gymnastics.

The gymnastics competition was one of elegance, tension and controversy. Arbitrarily judged sports are traditionally exposed to unresolvable argument, and there were many present at the Olympic Park Stadium who thought that Daniela Silivas of Romania, the silver medalist, was harshly treated. The two tiny girls had each given displays of astonishing virtuosity, as indeed had the 15-year-old Svetlana Boguinskaia, in third place.

Chouchounova and Silivas each scored six maximum 10 during the three days of the event, with two each on the final afternoon. Yet it seems far-fetched that the two should ultimately be divided by no more than 0.025 of a point, or less than one three-thousandth of their total score — 79.662 for the winner — by judges' discretion: the more so when it was evident that a Russian judge, the former competitor Nellie Kim, was low-marking Silivas; whose coach, Adrian Goreac, was afterwards critical of the scoring.

MODEL OF CONCENTRATION

Silivas throughout was brimming with confident self-awareness, an extrovert star, especially with the decline after injury of her even more youthful compatriot, the world champion Aurelia Dobre. Chouchounova, a year older than Silivas, was a model of concentration. She carried forward into the final day an advantage from the preliminaries of 0.050 points, which would prove invaluable.

Each had exotically athletic routines in the floor exercises, gaining 10. Silivas had opened with a 10 on asymmetric bars, and indeed was the higher scorer of the day. All was decided on the final vaulting horse. Silivas, jumping first, was marked at 9.975. Chouchounova, jumping last, needed a 10. With a handspring off the board and a backward twist

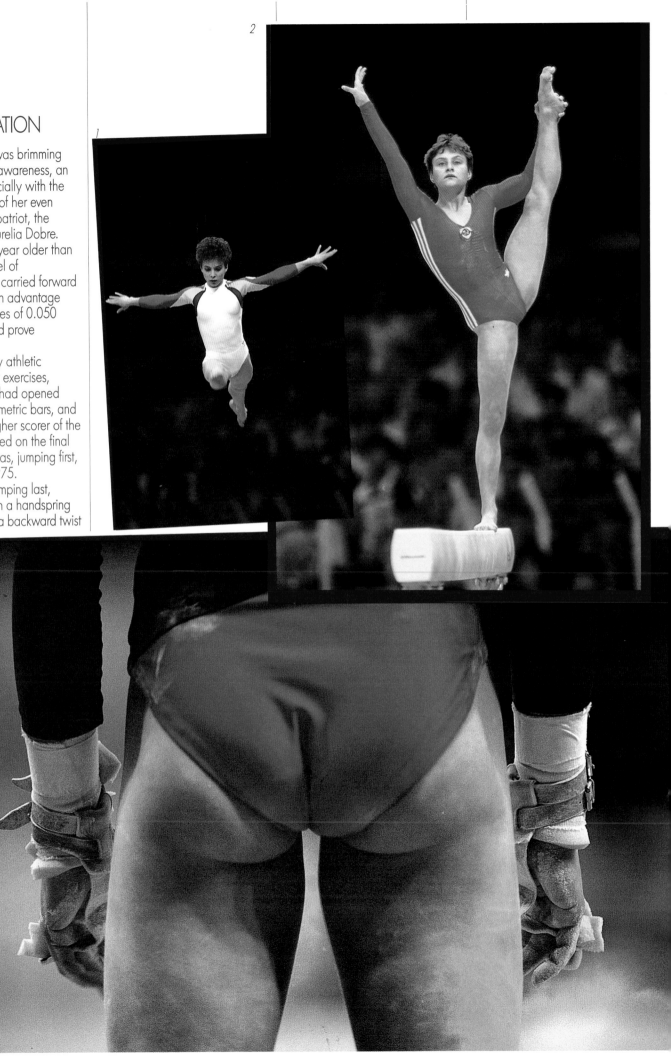

HARD PRESSED

Mota, the first Portuguese woman to win an Olympic gold medal, set the pace of the marathon from early on, but was hard pressed until about five miles (8 km) from the finish. Until the half-way stage there had been a dozen runners in the leading pack, but by the three-quarter mark of the 26-mile 385-yard race (42 km) there were only four left in the hunt: Mota, Lisa Martin of Australia, Kathrin Doerre of the GDR and Tatiana Polovinskaia of the Soviet Union. Soon the Russian faded, leaving three to dispute the medals. Mota made her critical move about two and a half miles from the finish, coming into one of the few downhill phases of the course."I just couldn't go with her" Martin said afterwards. Mota, the European champion of 1986, was nearly a minute slower than the winning time of Joan Benoit in Los Angeles, where she was third. She won in 2 hours 25 minutes 39 seconds. Martin and Doerre entered the stadium before Mota crossed the line, Martin taking the silver.

Ulf Timmermann of the GDR, the world record holder of the men's shot put, set a new Olympic record of 22.47 meters (73¾ feet) with his sixth throw: and had broken the record with his first, third and fifth throws. Randy Barnes, an un-tipped American, won the silver, and Werner Guenthoer of Switzerland, the 1987 world champion, the bronze.

off the horse, she got it. There had been earlier dissatisfaction with the judging. The United States women's team was penalized half a point that may have cost them the bronze medal, in a duel with the GDR, for a non-performing technical infringement spotted by one of the judges...from the GDR.

1. Daniela Silivas, queen of style and unlucky silver medalist in individual all-round gymnastics.
2. The superiority of Elena Chouchounova's expression on the beam foretells the result. She won.
3. Andrea Ladanyi of Hungary suffers a moment of self-doubt in the all-round final.
4. Svetlana Boguinskaia, rising young Soviet star, puts a final touch of resin on the asymetric bars.

1. Soviet attacker penetrates the United States defence at handball.
2. Reach for the sky. Peru versus China.
3. This Italian seems to find it more amusing than the rest.
4. Lamour of France rejoices at sabre silver medal.
5. Lamour of France records a hit in winning the sabre.
6. Get ready to take what's coming to you.
7. If you know the way, I'll follow. The 20 km walk.

UNEXPECTED FORCE

Kalusha Bwalya emerged as the unexpected force of the football tournament, as it reached the quarter final stage. A professional with Bruges in Belgium, Bwalya was the leading scorer in the first round, including a hat-trick against Italy during a remarkable 4-0 win for Zambia. It was the kind of reversal which football has come to expect intermittently with Italy, who had delayed the start of their league season so that their highly-paid players could compete.

Zambia's victory earned them a meeting with the Federal Republic of Germany, who would be without the suspended Mill. Italy, having already beaten Guatemala and Iraq, still qualified, to play Sweden, winners over the Federal Republic of Germany. The Soviet Union, held to a draw by Korea, led their group to earn a meeting with Australia, but the outstanding match of the last eight promised to be Brazil against Argentina, in Seoul. Peru confirmed their position as favorites in women's volleyball with a five-set victory during two hours and twenty minutes against the defending Olympic champions, China.

September 23 proved to be the end of the line for Pertti Karppinen of Finland, winner of the single sculls at the past three Games. He could only finish last in his semi-final, at the ripe old age of 35.

7

1. *Ecstasy for Uwe Dassler, 400 meters freestyle winner.*
2. *American back-slapping after 4 x 100 meters freestyle relay victory.*
3. *I can't believe it. Tania Dangalakova wins the 100 meters breaststroke.*

1

3

2

The essence of beauty and grace . . . speed
and agility from gymnastics and cycling.

1. Muscle at the ready. Johnson's eyes are transfixed on his goal.
2. Ready for anything, except the unexpected.
3. Johnson is airborne and already a quarter of a stride ahead coming out of the blocks at the start of the 100 meters final.
4. Has Ben Johnson spotted something wrong at the end of his record 100 meters? Carl Lewis seems questioning.
5. A lissom Lewis eases through 100 meters semi-final.

JOHNSON BRINGS CANADA'S FIRST GOLD

Ben Johnson of Canada upstaged his world record 100 meters of the 1987 world championships in Rome by running a phenomenal 9.79 secs. to take the Olympic title. The endless speculation on his superiority over Carl Lewis of America, the winner in Los Angeles was to take a dramatic twist 48 hours later, of which neither was aware.

With an explosive start, Johnson led from start to finish in a race in which the first four ran under 10 secs. Johnson improved his record by four hundredths; Lewis, who had run 9.3 when coming second in Rome, recorded a new American record of 9.2; Linford Christie of Britain established a new European and Commonwealth record of 9.99.

Lewis, as so often, was away poorly by comparison with his rival, and from then on his eyes were glancing right from lane three to lane six as Johnson thundered down the track ahead of him. So confident was Johnson that a few meters from the line he turned his head to the left, saw no-one, and raised his right arm in triumph: all of which must have cost him another couple of hundredths on his time. Johnson's win brought Canada's first gold medal of the Games, but it was to prove a temporary elation that would turn horribly sour. Other notable events at the Olympic Stadium were the new world record of Jackie Joyner Kersee in the heptathlon, with 7,291 points; a new Olympic triple jump record by Hristo Markov of Bulgaria; and the failure of Steve Cram of Britain to qualify for the semi-final of the men's 800 meters. Cram was bidding for a 800/1,500 double.

2

1

3

4

1. Jackie Joyner Kersee looks into the future, with a heavier than normal crystal ball.
2. Three in a row. Behmer, John and Schulz of the GDR chase heptathlon points in the 800 meters.
3. A stretch before the semi-final for Florence Griffith Joyner.
4. Florence Griffith Joyner strips for action.

1

1. Pain and pleasure for the FRG double sculls pair.
2. Whose right of way? Finn Class crews eye each other warily.
3. Is there no-one else in this race?
4. Daichi Suzuki celebrates 100 meters backstroke.
5. Michael Gross of the FRG is all power in winning the 200 meters butterfly.
6. Testing Archimedes's theory?

4

5

HAN RIVER REGATTA COURSE DOMINATED BY THE GDR

A busy day at the Han River Regatta Course was dominated by the German Democratic Republic, which won four of the seven finals decided. The particular surprise was the defeat of Michael Kolbe of the Federal Republic of Germany, five times the world champion, by Thomas Lange of the GDR in the single sculls, Eric Verdonk of New Zealand taking the bronze medal. The GDR also won the women's double sculls and women's and men's coxed fours. China had been two seconds clear with 500 meters to go of the 2 km course in the women's coxed fours, but were then overhauled. Ron ... Florijn and Nicolaas Rienks of the Netherlands won a thrilling men's double skulls from Switzerland and the Soviet Union, after the Soviets had their bow in front at the half-way mark. Steve Redgrave and Andrew Holmes, world champions in Copenhagen last year, overcame injury problems before the Games to be comfortable winners of the men's coxless pairs over their old rivals from Romania, Dragos Neagu and Danut Dobre, with Yugoslavia third.

6

3

4

6

7

8

PARK JONG-HOON, THE FIRST KOREAN MEDALIST IN GYMNASTICS

Soviet men dominated the individual apparatus events at the gymnastics hall, where Park Jong-hoon became the first Korean Republic winner of a gymnastics medal. A perfect second vault of 10 points gave him the bronze medal behind Lou Yun of China and Sylvio Kroll of GDR. Vladimir Artemov of the Soviet Union, who had earlier won team and all-round individual medals, became the first man of the Games with four golds when he won the horizontal bar and parallel bars. Matt Biondi achieved the same distinction in swimming, in which Kristin Otto of the GDR gained a fifth gold medal. For the second time in a week, a Bulgarian weightlifter was stripped of a gold medal, Anguel Guenchev, winner of the 65.75 kg (145 lbs) class, being found positive with furosemide, a drug that screens the use of steroids.

1. Kim Hagger of Britain gets high in the heptathlon long jump.
2. Anke Behmer leaps for heptathlon third place.
3. Spain and Brazil get in a twist.
4. The FRG team takes time off on the way to winning the equestrian three-day event.
5. Hristo Markov finds some triple jump leverage.
6. Alexandre Kovalenko reaching out in the triple jump.
7. Frictionless speed. Umaras of the Soviet Union wins the 4,000 meters individual pursuit.
8. A sprint to the finish.

THE LAUGHING PRINCESS

Florence Griffith — Joyner became the laughing princess of the Games when she ran the last quarter of the 100 meters final with the broadest of smiles. It was hardly surprising that she should win, following her exceptional world record during the American trials at Indianapolis in July, when her time of 10.49 secs was almost three tenths of a second faster than any woman had run before. That she should run in an Olympic final with such abandon, as though it were carnival time, was a reflection of her confidence.

By the 70 meter mark a smile was starting to play across her face. Within another 15 meters it had become a grin and before the finish she was waving her arms in delight. Evelyn Ashford, the champion of Los Angeles, could only glance across with a mixture of envy and admiration as she dipped at the line to get second place, a fraction in front of Heike Drechsler of the GDR.

The ebullient Joyner was handed a flag by Andre Phillips, her compatriot, who was still on the perimeter of the track following his victory in the men's 400 meters hurdles: a race which had seen Edwin Moses dethroned as twelve-year master of the event. For nine of those years Phillips had been pursuing Moses, his idol and his inspiration. Though Phillips was ranked number one in 1985 and 1986, he had never beaten Moses until this day, and he had to run an Olympic record of 47.19 secs. to do it. Moses's world record of 47.02 had stood since 1983.

At the age of 33, Moses had to relinquish his crown; Olympic champion of 1976 and 1984, world champion of 1983 and 1987. It had been one of the most dominating careers in the history of track and field. Now he had to accept a bronze medal, for in the last 50 meters a surge had carried Amadou Dia Ba of Senegal into second place.

4

5

6

1. Griffith-Joyner just can't help breaking records. This one's the 100 meters.
2. The laughing princess waves to the world.
3. Thanksgiving.
4. A third Olympic victory eludes Moses the master.
5. Andre Phillips (US) snatches the 400 meters hurdles from Amadou Ba (Senegal) and Ed Moses (US) ... and shows the flag.
6. Tears of triumph.

3

1. Blue water rhythm of the quadruple sculls.

2. The dinosaurs glide to the start of two kilometers of hell.

3. A Danish sculler is overcome as he crosses the finishing line.

4. Single Scullers under way.

5. Synchronized blades, matching puddles.

6. The Federal Republic of Germany crew jubilant after victory in the eights.

7. Abbagnale brothers of Italy and their coxswain, Di Capua, find relief and joy in the coxed pairs victory.

7

1

2

THE ALL-POWERFUL ROWING TEAM OF THE GDR

For the second consecutive day the all-powerful rowing team of the GDR took four of the seven gold medals, for a total of eight out of fourteen. It was their women who led the way, winning all three of

7

6

their finals. Jutta Behrendt took the single sculls, ahead of Anne Marden of the U.S. and Magdalena Gueorguieva, the Bulgarian world champion. The women's quadruple sculls and eights also went to the GDR, as did the men's coxless fours.

Italy won two golds at the Han River regatta course, the Abbagnale brothers, Carmine and Giuseppe, repeating their victory of 1984, and younger brother Agostino being a member of the winning quadruple sculls team. In a thrilling finish to the men's eights, the Federal Republic of Germany won by half a length from the Soviet Union, who beat the United States by a canvas.

The performance of Steve Redgrave

1

and Andy Holmes of Britain was without parallel in modern rowing. Having won the coxless pairs the day before, they were challenging the Abbagnales, four times world champions, in the coxed event. Six races in a week had sapped some of the power from the British pair, and they had to be content with the bronze behind the GDR: a nonetheless unique double medal.

2

3

CHRIS EVERT LOST THE CHANCE OF ONE LAST MOMENT OF GLORY

In one of several surprise defeats in the tennis competition, Chris Evert lost the chance of one last moment of glory, in an Olympic Games, when she was beaten by the unseeded Raffaella Reggi of Italy in three sets. At the age of 33, time had moved on for the American winner of 18 grand slam singles titles.

Daniela Silivas of Romania had some compensation for her controversial defeat in the women's all-round gymnastics when she won three golds in the separate apparatus event: beam, asymmetric bars and floor exercises.

The dreams of Zambia, outsiders in the football competition, who had put four goals past Italy, ended with their four-goal defeat at the hands of the Federal Republic of Germany, for whom Juergen Klinsmann scored three goals. The Netherlands, the Korean hosts, Australia and Britain advanced to the semi-finals of the women's hockey. Kim Jae-yup gained the second gold medal for the host country when, on the day of Korea's traditional Chusok holiday, he won the 60 kg (132¼ lbs.). bantamweight title in judo. Silver medalist four years ago, Kim defeated Kevin Asano of the United States, who had eliminated the favorite, Shinji Hosokawa of Japan, the man who beat Kim in Los Angeles.

The degradation of the weightlifting competition continued. Following the positive dope test on two Bulgarians and the withdrawal of their team, Kalman Czengeri of Hungary and Fernando Mariaca of Spain also had positive tests.

1. Blue water rhythm of the quadruple sculls.
2. Digging water. Redgrave and Holmes of Britain on the way to coxless pairs victory.
3. Raffaella Reggi (Italy) gets two-handed satisfaction in beating Cris Evert (US).
4. ... and senses a gold medal coming his way.
5. Kim Jae-yup (KOR) jockeys with his opponent.
6. Well dressed for dressage. FRG (winners), Switzerland and Canada.
7. Daniela Silivas of Romania, exotic champion of the floor exercises.
8. Searching for a landing. Garrison-Steves of America.

1. Grant of Britain covers both sides of the argument.

2. Avdeyenko of the Soviet Union in the clear … and pleased about it.

3. Tessa Sanderson (GBR), in pain from injury, fails to qualify.

4. Povarnitsyn (URS) gives thanks for clearing the bar.

5. Dietmar Moegenburg winces at the effort.

6. Tapio Korjus of Finland lines up his winning javelin throw.

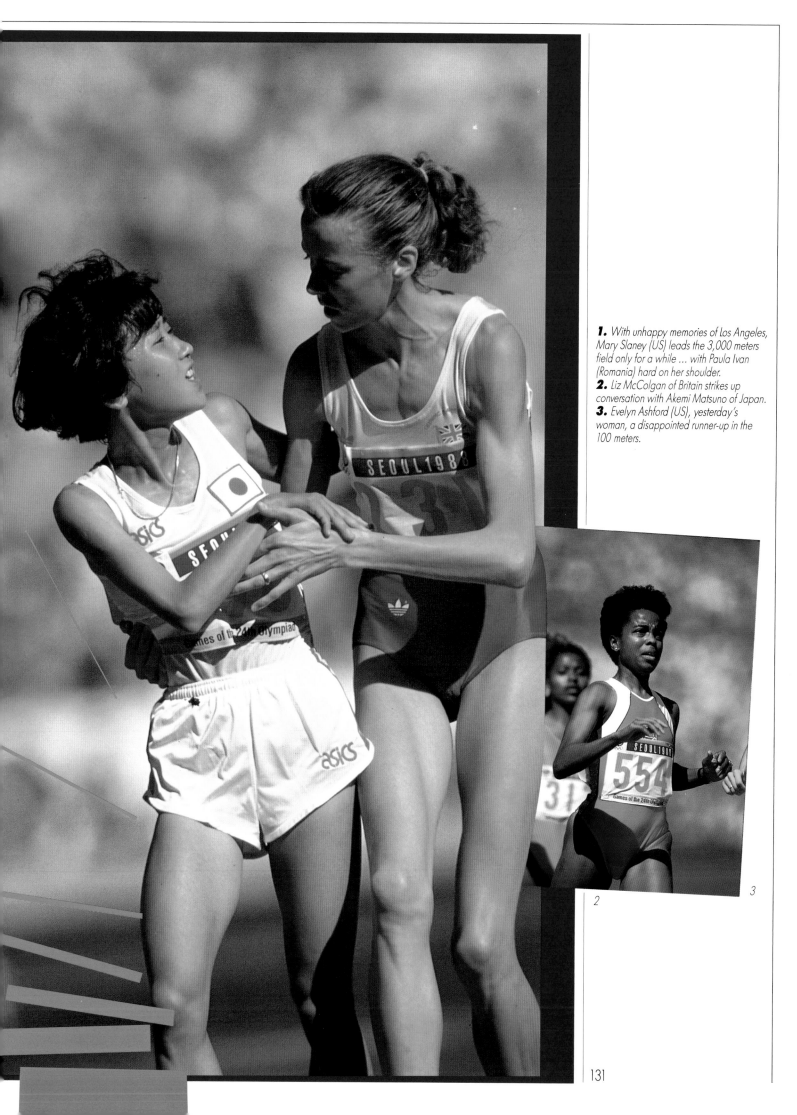

1. With unhappy memories of Los Angeles, Mary Slaney (US) leads the 3,000 meters field only for a while ... with Paula Ivan (Romania) hard on her shoulder.
2. Liz McColgan of Britain strikes up conversation with Akemi Matsuno of Japan.
3. Evelyn Ashford (US), yesterday's woman, a disappointed runner-up in the 100 meters.

2

3

1

2

PAUL ERENG WINS AN OLYMPIC GOLD WITH BIBLICAL SIMPLICITY

With almost biblical simplicity, Paul Ereng, as a boy a cow-herd, came down from the high plains of Kenya to win an Olympic gold medal. If we were astonished by the improbability of his victory, he himself was reeling in a daze of disbelief.

He not only beat Joachim Cruz, the defending 800 meters champion, but also the legendary Said Aouita, who had been telling anyone who cared to listen that he regarded himself as unbeatable. So, frankly, had we. Until along came the incredible Ereng. Never having run an 800 until

3

4

5

1. Roger Kingdom (US) leads Colin Jackson (GBR), right, on the way to gold and silver in the high hurdles.
2. Strapping on his thigh could not help an injured Aouita fulfil his ambitions.
3. Brothers-in-arm. Boutaib of Morocco, the 10,000 meters winner, left, with Kimeli of Kenya, third, and Antibo of Italy, second.
4, 5. Paul Ereng, the Kenyan who came from nowhere to win the 800 meters, pips the defending champion Joachim Cruz. Said Aouita, third, is out of the picture. Peter Elliott (418) was fourth.

earlier this year, this 21-year-old on a scholarship to the University of Virginia at Charlottesville is yet another phenomenal Kenyan runner. Mike Koskei, the chief national middle-distance coach, considers that Ereng can ultimately achieve a time of around 1 min 39 secs, some two seconds faster than Sebastian Coe's seven year old world record.

Running through from the back of

1. Petra Felke of the GDR eyes the horizon for winning javelin throw.
2. Monique Knol is happy after winning the road race.
3. Sigrun Wodars of the GDR conquers the 800 meters field.
4, 5. Carl Lewis takes off ... and touches down in long jump victory.
6. So near yet so far. Kim Gallager (US), third in the 800 meters.
7. Sergei Litvinov in pensive mood for the hammer throw.

the field off the crown of the final bend, Ereng swept past a host of famous names, surging to the front ahead of Cruz with 45 meters or so to go. His winning time was 1:43.45, and that of Cruz 1:43.90. Aouita had to be content with third place. Reluctantly. He had been running with strapped thighs.

Part of this romantic story is the sacrifice made by Ereng's colleague, Nixon Kiprotich; who, in a plan devised by Koskei, set out to establish such a pace that Cruz and Barbosa of Brazil would have no finishing kick. The Brazilians had simultaneously planned to wring the speed out of Aouita by the 600 mark: thus opening the way for the emergence of the least heralded hero since Bikela won his first Olympic marathon.

Yet the real story lay in how Ereng came to be in Seoul. Born among the Turkana tribe in a remote village in the Rift Valley, without electricity or roads, he had won a place at a school for the under-privileged in Nairobi, been spotted by an American talent scout, given an athletic scholarship in Virginia ...

5

2

1

7

136

and only won a place on the Kenyan team because a Nairobi newspaper spotted his results among Reuters agency tapes, and the athletic federation sent him a ticket to fly home for the trials, in which he finished third. Formerly a 400 meters runner, he had been converted by his coach at Charlottesville, yet had run only two 800 races of consequence. ''I had no sort of record,'' he admitted afterwards, gazing uncomprehendingly at a huge audience of the world's press. Almost while we were still talking to Ereng, there was another memorable race taking place out on the track. Moulay Brahim Boutaib stole the Moroccan limelight from Aouita by running away with the men's 10,000 meters — after Kipkemboi Kimeli of Kenya and Salvatore Antibo of Italy had set the early pace.

Boutaib then moved ahead, and ran without falter to the finish to win in the fourth fastest time ever, 27 mins. 21.46 secs.: some 17 seconds faster than Viren's Olympic record of 1972. Antibo passed Kimeli on the last lap to take the silver.

In other finals at the Olympic Stadium, Carl Lewis retained his long jump title, while Roger Kingdom of the USA became the first to retain the high hurdles, when he won in a new record of 12.98 secs. Britain had, for them, a rare three finalists, with Colin Jackson taking the silver ahead of Tony Cambell (USA).

A SECOND GOLD FOR THE HOST NATION

The Korean two-day Chusok holiday saw the host nation win a second gold medal in judo, when Lee Kyung-keun won the 65 kg (143¼ lbs.) title. He defeated Janusz Pawlowski of Poland at the Changchung Stadium, where there was standing room only.

1. Bottoms up.
2. Shared effort.
3. With such a small ball, you've got to watch it.
4. Yuriy Sedykh puts a swing into silver medal hammer throw.
5. United States goalkeeper makes a diving save against Britain.
6. A national hero Kyung-keun Lee, judo champion of 65 kg. (143¼ lbs.) division
7. Udo Quellmalz of the GDR is upended by Yosuke Yamamoto of Japan.

In an extraordinary finish to the women's individual cycling road race, 45 riders swept down simultaneously on the finishing line. After officials had studied the photo-finish of the 82 km. race, the gold was awarded to Monique Knol, a 24-year-old Dutch school teacher, with Jutta Niehaus of Federal Republic of Germany in second place and Laima Zilporitee of the Soviet Union third — all in the same time of 2 hours 00.52 secs.

The relentless swimming pair, Otto and Biondi, took their golden tally to six and five respectively.

1. *A forest of wheels.*
2. *A stretch before the off.*

1

1. *This means business. American prepares for individual road race.*
2. *l. to r. Dr Robert Dugal (Canada), medical commission; Prince Alexandre de Merode, chairman of medical commission; Michele Verdier, IOC press director; and Raymond Gafner, chief administrator of the IOC, announce the suspension of Johnson.*
3. *The man behind the news. Charlie Francis, coach to Ben Johnson.*
4. *Was it worth it?*
5. *Alone with the birds and reflections. Carl Lewis.*

COMITE INTERNATIONAL OLYMPIQUE
REF. No. PR/71 /MPV
Seoul, 26th September 1988

PRESS RELEASE

RECOMMENDATION OF THE IOC MEDICAL COMMISSION TO THE IOC EXECUTIVE BOARD UNANIMOUSLY APPROVED BY THE IOC EXECUTIVE BOARD

The urine sample of Ben Johnson (Canada-Athletics-100m) collected on Saturday, 24th September 1988 was found to contain the metabolites of a banned substance namely Stanozolol (anabolic steroid).

The IOC Medical Commission discussed all arguments presented by the Canadian Delegation, especially the statement that the substance in question might have been administered after the competition by a third party.
The steroid profile however is not consistent with such a claim.
The IOC Medical Commission recommends the following sanction:
— disqualification of this competitor from the Games of the XXIVth Olympiad in Seoul.
The decision remains independent of any sanction which the International Federation concerned may wish to apply in accordance with its own regulations.

DAY 11

BEN JOHNSON'S IMPENDING HUMILIATION

On Sunday evening and in the early hours of Monday morning, the tenth day of the Games, there began to emerge the worst scandal in Olympic history. The drugs test on Ben Johnson, winner of the 100 meters in the most publicized event of 1988, had proved positive, and at 2 a.m. the Canadian Olympic Committee was notified to attend the confirmatory test later that morning.

All Monday night rumors of Johnson's impending humiliation hummed on agency wires around the world. Before light on Tuesday, Johnson was already on an airplane to New York, hustled out of Seoul like a criminal. The sporting world, indeed everybody, was stunned. When Prince Alexandre de

Merode, chairman of the Medical Commission of the International Olympic Committee, made the formal announcement to a packed press and television gathering at 10 a.m. there was a chilling finality to the statement. The profile of Stanozolol, an anabolic steroid agent, in Johnson's urine sample was unequivocally positive. A Canadian defense that a soft drink consumed by Johnson prior to the race could have been sabotaged was wholly outside the scientific evidence, stated Dr Robert Dugal, a specialist on the drugs sub-commission. The whole of Canada winced under the shock, not least the many of Jamaican stock, for whom

Johnson was their particular hero. Jean Charest, the sports minister, announced that the 26-year-old Johnson was banned for life from all Canadian teams and from government financial assistance. The grief for Johnson's family would be harrowing.

Carol Anne Letheren, the chief of the Canadian team, whose job it had been to take back from Johnson the gold medal in the middle of Monday night, said with emotion: "We are acutely aware how devastating this news will be to millions of people. I wish there was something we could do to relieve that pain, but there is not. I assure them that their heartbreak is shared by all of the Canadian Olympic team."

That tarnished medal would now pass to Carl Lewis, defeated in the show-down three days previously, and would restore the possibility of Lewis uniquely repeating his four gold medals of 1984. He had already become the first man ever to retain the long jump title. Meanwhile, the Olympic community was bracing itself to

2

3

4

141

absorb the shock. The almost unanimous view among members of the IOC and International Federations was that the incident was to the long-term benefit of the Olympic Games. It would perhaps frighten those who contemplated cheating like Johnson. Apart from the sporting shame, the announcement had stressed the side-effect danger from Stanozolol of cancer of the liver.

Juan Antonio Samaranch, the IOC president, who had warned, in his opening address to the Session two weeks beforehand, that "doping is death", now expressed optimism. "The bad news we can transform into good news" he said. "This is not a disaster, for it shows that the IOC is very serious, and that we are winning the battle for a clean Games. The gap between our aims and those who are cheating is narrowing. I am very sorry for Johnson, who is a great athlete, but he is not the only person we have to blame."

Marat Gramov, the Soviet sports minister and a new IOC member, said gravely: "We are all involved in this problem, and we have to find a collective solution." James Worrall, Canada's senior IOC member, deeply saddened by such an event after 20 years on the IOC and over 50 years in sport, said: "Ben is basically a decent but simple young man. We have to find the involvement of others." An important step in the move towards a stronger stance on drugs among Olympic sports came with Samaranch's appointment to the Medical Commission, a year previously, of Dr Arne Ljungqvist of Sweden, a member of the medical commission of the International Amateur Athletic Federation. When Samaranch and Dr Primo Nebiolo, the IAAF president, briefly discussed the impending crisis before the announcement, there was instant resolve between them. While the shadow of suspicion would now hover over every

medalist, the fear of detection and disgrace would, it was hoped, prove a massive deterrent. Wajid Ali of Pakistan, the fifth longest serving IOC member, said when congratulating Samaranch: "You have given a fine example at the top."

In the women's tennis Steffi Graf had an unexpectedly long match against Larissa Savchenko of the Soviet Union, winning 6-2, 4-6, 6-3. In the semi-final she would meet Zina Garrison, who defeated Pam Shriver, with the other match being between Gabriela Sabatini and Manuela Maleeva of Bulgaria. The men's individual cycling road race was won by Olaf Ludwig of the GDR, ahead of Brend Groene and Christian Henn, both of FRG.

1. All-out serve from Gabriela Sabatini of Argentina.
2. The elegance and power of Sabatini.
3, 4. Stefan Edberg, the Wimbledon champion, shows his class on forehand volley and smash.
5. Tim Mayotte (US) controls a forehand volley at the net.

1

4

2

3

5

1. *Irresistible force, immovable object.*
2. *I'm not sure my knees can take it.*
3. *One big heave and we're there. Andrew Davies of Britain.*
4, 5. *The relief of success. Zakarevitch of the Soviet Union.*

145

1. Prikeba Phipps (US) directs the action.
2. This is more difficult than it looks. Xiong of China on the high bar.
3. Missed it. Ni Shiwei of China.
4. Hungary aim at the United States goal.
5. Out of my way. China versus Yugoslavia.
6. The ball was there a moment ago. Yugoslavia versus China.
7. A little bit left behind the fleets.

EXCELLENCE TO BRIGHTEN THE GLOOM

3

There was excellence on this eleventh day of the Games to brighten the gloom. Greg Louganis came from behind on his final dive to overtake Ni Xiong of China in the platform diving. Thus he became the first man to win both diving titles in successive Games. With a reverse three-and-a-half somersault from the tuck position, Louganis scored 86.70 points. He had needed 86.57 to win.

With a silver medal in 1976, when he was a 16-year-old at Montreal, Louganis had five medals to match those of Klaus Dibasi of Italy — who was there at the Chamshil

4

Pool to see his record emulated. In women's basketball, Yugoslavia and the United States reached the final. With only seconds of the match remaining, Yugoslavia beat Australia on a single basket by 57-56. The scorer was Andjelija Arbutina. In the other semi-final, the U.S. women overpowered their traditional rivals, the USSR, by 102-88. The last time they had met was in 1976, when Soviet Union had won to take the gold medal.

5

7

147

DAY12

3

1. Steve Lewis glances left, and sees he has beaten the 400 meters world record holder, Butch Reynolds ... and has time for reflection.
2. Outjumped ... Soviet girls happy with their basketball victory over Australia.
3. The Soviet defense of the basket, versus USA.

USA RECEIVE A SECOND AND MORE EMPHATIC BEATING

The United States had waited sixteen years to gain revenge on the Soviet Union for their first and only defeat in men's basketball, in a disputed 1972 final. What they received was a second and more emphatic beating.

The loss in Munich had been controversial, the Soviet Union winning on a last-minute basket. This time there could be no argument, for the U.S. were never in front again from the time they led 4-3, and finally went down 82-76. It was only their second defeat in 87 Olympic match-ups, and the first time they had not reached the final. On Friday, the Soviets would meet Yugoslavia, who defeated Australia 91-70, having earlier beaten the Soviets in the first round. The Soviets controlled the pace of the game against America, and led 47-37 at half-time. In the second half, the Americans closed at one stage to 59-57, but the Soviets responded with six in a row. Their leading scorer, with 28, was Rimas Kourtinaitis, with Sharunas Marchulionis contributing 19, the same score David Robinson had for the U.S.

1

2

149

A BETTER STORY OVER AT THE OLYMPIC STADIUM

It was a better story for the U.S. over at the Olympic Stadium, where they took the first three places in the men's 400 meters and first two in the 200. In both there was an upset. Steve Lewis, the world junior record holder and at 19 the least experienced of the three Americans, won the gold medal ahead of Butch Reynolds, recent breaker of Lee Evans's 20-year-old world record in Mexico City.

Lewis finished in 43.87 secs., one hundredth of a second off Evans's time, which remains as the Olympic record. Reynolds could run only 43.93 in second place, compared with his 43.29 in Zurich; Danny Everett took the bronze.

Joe DeLoach's 200 meters victory robbed Carl Lewis of the possibility of repeating his quadruple gold of 1984: the 100 meters disqualification of Johnson having restored that. Although DeLoach, 21, ran a new Olympic record of 19.75 secs., there was evidence that Carl was feeling the effects of the long jump event. In the last few meters he visibly slowed, his stride shortening. He had had a slight lead coming off the turn, but could not hold it. Robson Silva of Brazil took the bronze.

Yet there was the risk that Johnson's disgrace was over shadowing the excellence of the greatest athlete since Owens. Lewis may engender,

for all his genius, a disaffection with the American public, yet he is the supreme natural runner. It was his bowing to public opinion, and taking all six jumps in the long jump

rather than merely one, as he had done in Los Angeles, that possibly cost him the 200 gold. That certainly was the opinion of Tom Tellez, his coach. "I didn't tell him not to jump all six" Tellez said, "but I know that the combination of eight races in the sprints and nine run-ups in the jump was too much for him."

1. Daley Thompson begins the defence of his Decathlon title with the 100 meters, first event on the first day ... and is quickly away.
2. Sergei Bubka, the pole vault champion, was constantly irritated by interruptions across the run up for medal presentations.
3. Cushioned landing. Earl Bell (US) touches down in pole vault.

1

2

3

1. *A face in the dark. Keriuki and Keoch, in shadow, poised to strike for gold and silver in the steeplechase.*
2. *Shadows lengthen. A semi-final of the 5,000 meters.*
3. *Carl Lewis coasts through the 200 heats.*
4. *On guard ... Attack!*

2

3

The schedule between long jump and 200 heats had been tighter than in Los Angeles; and after winning the jump on the fourth leap Lewis had slightly hurt an ankle on the fifth. Yet he had run an American record in the 100 of 9.92, bettered only by Johnson's run in Rome the previous year and by his disqualified time of Saturday; had leaped the sixth farthest jump ever with 8.72 meters (28 ft. 6 in.); and run the fourth fastest 200 with 19.79. "He is phenomenal," Tellez said.

The Soviet Union had a clean sweep in the pole vault. Bubka, the strongest favorite in the entire Games, cleared 5.90 meters (19 ft. 4 in.), which is modest for him, Gataoulline taking the silver with 5.85 (19 ft. 2 in.) and Egorov the bronze with 5.80 (19 ft.). All three beat the 1980 Olympic record of 5.78 (18 ft. 11 1/2 in.) set by Kozakiewicz of Poland, but were irritated by constant interruptions across the run-up due to medal ceremonies.

In one of the closest finishes of any Games, Debbie Flintoff-King of Australia held off the might of Eastern Europe to win the women's 400 meters hurdles by a hundredth of a second in 53.17 secs.. Tatiana Ledovskaia of the Soviet Union was second and Ellen Fiedler of GDR third. Sabina Busch, the world record holder, could finish only fourth.

EXCITEMENT IN THE MEN'S HOCKEY

There was excitement in the men's hockey semi-finals. The Netherlands led the Federal Republic of Germany by a goal at half time, Crucg having scored after 10 minutes, and Germany's goalkeeper Frank having saved a penalty shot by Koorjman. The Germans controlled the second half and Reck scored twice to steer them to a second consecutive final. In 1984 they lost to Pakistan, having won the title in 1972. Britain, two up against Australia, the World Cup holders, were pinned back to 2-2, but scored the winner with a few minutes to spare. In handball, the Korean and Soviet teams echoed the performances of their women counterparts by reaching the final. Though losing 23-20 to Spain, the Koreans still won their group. Stefan Edberg, the Wimbledon champion, lost his semi-final in tennis to Miloslav Mecir of Czechoslovakia in a five set battle, Mecir critically breaking service in the fifth game of the final set. Tim Mayotte (U.S.A.) beat Brad Gilbert (U.S.A.) in the other semi-final in straight sets. Steffi Graf and Claudia Kohde-Kilsch unexpectedly lost their doubles semi-final to the Czechoslovakian pair, Jana Novotna and Helena Sukova, in straight sets.

1. *Jarryd of Sweden waits to receive.*
2. *Big hitter.*
3. *Steffi Graf covers all angles.*
4. *Waiting for the action.*
5. *Doug Robbins (US) in difficulty on a run-down against Japan.*
6. *What sort of game is this?*
7. *Demonstration sport shows the flag.*

4

5

6

7

DAY**13**

KOREA ALIGHT WITH HAPPINESS

There may not have been quite the same frenzy in the streets as when Argentina won the world football championship in Buenos Aires in 1978, but the Republic of Korea was alight with happiness at their first Olympic victory in a team sport. Amid emotional scenes at the Suwon Gymnasium, 40 kilometers from Seoul, the under-sized and under-estimated Korean women's handball team defeated the Soviet Union 21-19.

The Soviets were the reigning world champions, and had a substantial advantage in both height and weight. The Koreans responded with speed and tactics to outwit the opposition. They, and a good many others, burst into tears of joy at the final whistle. With ten minutes to go, the Soviets had led for the first time by 17-16. Soon,

Lim Mi-kyung leveled the score, and Kim Hyun-mee began a three-goal rally which gave the Koreans a commanding 20-17 lead. When the Soviets came back to 20-18, Kim Myung-soon restored the margin with less than two minutes remaining; and there was time for the Soviets to score only once more.

The defeat pushed the Soviets into the bronze medal position behind Norway, which took the silver on goal difference. The Soviet Union had won the first two gold medals when the sport was introduced in 1976, and did not participate in 1984.

In women's basketball, the United States women's team made some amends for the defeat the day before of their men's team by the Soviet Union when they beat Yugoslavia 77-70 for the gold medal. The American women had won their first gold medal in Los Angeles without the presence of the socialist countries. Teresa Edwards, who played in that victory, was now the inspiration against Yugoslavia, scoring 18 points, with 14 of them coming in the second half.

1. Tears of triumph. Korean women's handball team weep unashamedly.
2. Somebody finds their team-mates rather boring. USA v. Yugoslavia.

1. *An easy run for Florence in the 200 heats.*
2. *Set for the start of the 200 meters.*
3. *Leslie Ann Skeete (GBR) going a treat.*
4. *Eyes down. Start of the women's 100 meters hurdles.*
5. *Florence Griffith-Joyner.*
6. *Oblivious to a global audience, Flojo takes a rest.*
7. *Kicking sand. Jackie Joyner-Kersee wins the long jump.*

1

4

3

2

FLORENCE AND JACKIE SWEEP ALL BEFORE THEM

It was a day of dominance for the U.S. women at the Olympic Stadium, where Florence Griffith-Joyner and Jackie Joyner-Kersee swept all before them. Griffith-Joyner, who had set a world record in the 100 meters at the U.S. trials and won the gold medal in Seoul, now set two world records on the way to winning the 200 meters. Having improved Marita Koch's record of 21.71 secs. with a semi-final time of 21.56, Griffith-Joyner improved on this less than two hours later with a stunning 21.34. As in her 100 meter race, she crossed the line almost casually, wreathed in smiles. On the medal rostrum she wept tears. Grace Jackson of Jamaica and Heike Drechsler of the GDR took second and third places respectively.

Earlier that morning, Griffith-Joyner's sister-in-law had added the long jump title to the heptathlon. Joyner-Kersee came from behind with an Olympic record of 7.40 meters (24 ft. 4 in.) to leave Drechsler with the silver medal. Galina Tchistiakova of the Soviet Union, the world record

7

5

6

holder, could do no better than take the bronze.

159

1

2

For much of the past twelve years the decathlon event, the most severe all-round test in track and field, had been dominated by Daley Thompson of Britain. Since the European Championships of 1978, when he finished second, he had claimed two Olympic, two European, three Commonwealth and one World Championship crown. His first major defeat had come at the World Championship of 1987, and now came another. Carrying an injury, as he did the year before, he could finish no higher than fourth. The unheralded winner was Christian Schenk of the GDR, with his compatriot Torsten Voss, the world champion, second, and Dave Steen, of Canada, third. Steen overhauled Thompson in the final event, the 1,500 meters. The

1. Breaking point. Daley Thompson's pole cannot take the strain.
2. Dave Steen of Canada, bronze medalist in decathlon, who moved ahead of Thompson on the final event, 1,500 meters.
3. Pole and vaulter part company.
4. Plaziat of France clears the bar in the decathlon, but has sliped from among the leaders.
5. The message from Seoul

second day of this gruelling competition had run for 13 hours, ending at 9:25 p.m., some three hours behind schedule, due to an extended pole vault event; and thereby delaying a dress rehearsal of the Closing Ceremony.

3

2

Schenk, a 23-year-old medical student from Rostock, had been in sixth place after the first three events, but then set a decathlon record for the high jump with 2.27 meters (7 ft. 5 in.), worth 1,061 points. At the end of the first day, after five events, the order was Schenk, Plaziat (France) and Thompson. On his first attempt at the pole vault, at 4.70 meters (15 ft. 5 in.), Thompson's pole had snapped, injuring his hand, and though he recovered, he dropped to fourth place. Tim Bright of America vaulted 5.70 (18 ft. 8 in.) to bring himself into contention. A personal best in the Javelin brought Thompson back to third place, but, with Schenk and Voss safe as the leaders, Steen's 1,500 meter run denied the double gold medalist a unique third medal.

1. Schenk bites his lip as he goes for the penultimate event of the decathlon.
2. The end of an era. Thompson, twice Olympic champion, his fingers lacerated from the pole vault accident and his injured · thigh heavily bandaged, hangs his head at the end of the 1,500 meters, pipped for the bronze. Schenk, the winner, has his head partly hidden. Voss, third, kneels with exhaustion.
3. British to the core.

1

1. *Mon Dieu. C'est terrible!*
2. *A roar of success from Zaweija (FRG).*
3. *Nerlinger (FRG) nearly buckles under load.*
4. *Kobayashi of Japan gets the golden handshake in wrestling 48 kg class.*
5. *Khadartsev (URS) gets his legs in a twist against Ota of Japan.*

2

3

4

5

DOES TENNIS NEED THE OLYMPIC GAMES?

The critics said that the Olympic Games did not need tennis, and that tennis did not need the Olympic Games. Nothing could have been more appropriate than Miloslav Mecir of Czechoslovakia should win the first men's singles title in 64 years, beating Tim

3

1

2

4

Mayotte of the United States 3-6, 6-2, 6-4, 6-2. The objective to achieve the return of tennis to the Olympics was a priority of Philippe Chartier of France when he became president of the international federation eleven years ago. He wanted to demonstrate that tennis was not the preserve of the capitalist nations, and to promote the game more widely throughout Africa and Asia: the responsibility of any federation. Many governments, being the sole source of national funding for sport, will not assist any sport which is not included in the Olympic program.

DAY 14

Mecir had wanted to win the title to promote his country more than himself. Stefan Edberg had talked of the mood of the Games being similar to the Davis Cup. It is an irony that while many champions in Seoul, whether from capitalist or socialist countries, were performing for the enhancement of their careers, those in tennis were playing for no reward other than the honor; the truest Olympic spirit. The last player to win an Olympic tennis title was Vincent Richards of America, in Paris in 1924. Tennis had been only a demonstration sport in 1984. Mecir lost the first set, twice surrendering his service as Mayotte won four of the last five games, but he took Mayotte's service in the opening game of the second set and was in control thereafter. In their first competitive meeting, Mayotte soon realized he must attack the net to win, but Mecir foiled him with telling passing shots and lobs. Pam Shriver and Zina Garrison of America beat Jana Novotna and Helena Sukova of Czechoslovakia to take the women's doubles. The Czechoslovakians saved five match points before losing 10-8 in the final set.

6

7

1. Lisa Garrison prepares to serve ... and smash.
2. The moment of the supreme consegration.
3. Tim Mayotte winds up in the men's final.
4. It's a warm job.
5. Dead center. A smash from Mecir.
6. Which way did that one go?
7. Miloslav Mecir, first singles champion for 64 years, looks happy about it ... congratulates Mayotte ... and receives his medal.

EXHILARATING KENYAN RUNNERS

For the third time in Olympic history, Kenya took first and second place in the 3,000 meters steeplechase. Their exhilarating runners were a feature of the track and field events, and now it was Julius Kariuki and Peter Koech who dominated the race. Kariuki set a new Olympic record of 8 mins. 5.51 secs., the second fastest ever run and only a tenth of a second outside the ten year old record of his countryman Henry Rono. The Olympic record of Anders Garderud of Sweden had stood since 1976. Koech was just over a second behind Kariuki, with Mark Rowland of Britain an unexpected third, a further second behind. Elizabeth McColgan of Britain had been predicted to make a race of it in the women's 10,000 meters, and she did just that, leading for much of the 25 laps. In the final 200 meters, Olga Bondarenko of the Soviet Union sprinted past her to win in 31 mins. 5.21 secs.. Elena Joupieva of the Soviet Union was third. Ingrid Kristiansen of Norway, 32, the world record holder, who had set the fastest time of a new Olympic event in the heats with 31:44.69, had to drop out after less than three kilometers with a foot injury, sustained in the heats. Bondarenko's time was 52 seconds behind Kristiansen's world best. Carl Lewis's hopes of a third gold medal evaporated when the United States 4 x 100 meters relay team was disqualified in the heats for a faulty baton change. Louise Ritter of the United States won the women's high jump with an Olympic record of 2.03 meters (6 ft. 8 in.). She and Stefka Konstadinova of Bulgaria, who set a world record of 2.09 (6 ft. 10 1/4 in.) in the world championships of 1987, had tied with three failures each at 2.03. In a jump-off, Ritter cleared the height. Jordanka Donkova of Bulgaria, the favorite, set an Olympic record of 12.38 secs. in winning the women's 100 meters hurdles.

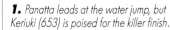

1. Panatta leads at the water jump, but Keriuki (653) is poised for the killer finish.
2. A long way to go yet. The start of the 50 km walk.
3. Jordanka Donkova, the winner, leads Gloria Siebert, runner up, in the hurdles final.
4. Well built for the job.
5. Li McColgan of Britain, narrowly beaten on the run-in of the 10,000 meters, is congratulated by John Anderson, her coach.
6. Sisters of compassion.

2

3

6

THE SOVIET UNION TURNED THE TABLES

Beaten by Yugoslavia four times in five meetings in recent months, including the opening game of the preliminary round in Seoul, the Soviet Union turned the tables in the men's basketball final, with a

76-63 victory. Alexandre Gomelsky, the 60-year-old Soviet coach who had guided their team at six Olympic Games, was tossed in the air in celebration at the finish. Raimondas Martchioulenis was the leading Soviet scorer with 21 points, while Drazen Petrovic scored 24 for the losers. The United States men's volleyball team was far too strong for Brazil. Aurelio Miguel won Brazil's first gold medal in Seoul, and their first ever in judo, when he defeated Marc Meiling of Federal Republic of Germany by a half point in the 95 kg. (209 1/2 lbs.) division.

1

5

3

1. They shall not pass.
2. Australia find it hot going ... occasionally lose the ball ... in spite of their half-time instructions the Korean team lose the final.
3. Basketball drama. Yugoslavia attack the Soviet net in the men's final.
4. Louise Ritter, surprise high jump winner, finds the occasion stressful.
5. Soviet satisfaction.

2

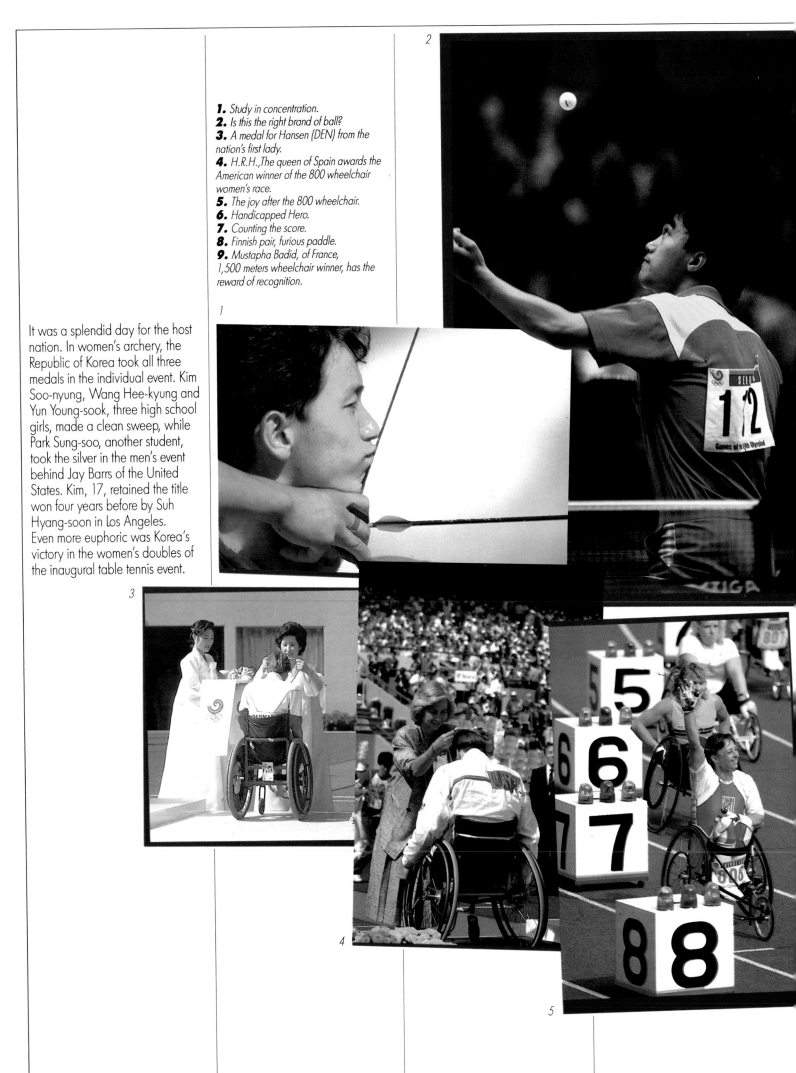

1. *Study in concentration.*
2. *Is this the right brand of ball?*
3. *A medal for Hansen (DEN) from the nation's first lady.*
4. *H.R.H.,The queen of Spain awards the American winner of the 800 wheelchair women's race.*
5. *The joy after the 800 wheelchair.*
6. *Handicapped Hero.*
7. *Counting the score.*
8. *Finnish pair, furious paddle.*
9. *Mustapha Badid, of France, 1,500 meters wheelchair winner, has the reward of recognition.*

It was a splendid day for the host nation. In women's archery, the Republic of Korea took all three medals in the individual event. Kim Soo-nyung, Wang Hee-kyung and Yun Young-sook, three high school girls, made a clean sweep, while Park Sung-soo, another student, took the silver in the men's event behind Jay Barrs of the United States. Kim, 17, retained the title won four years before by Suh Hyang-soon in Los Angeles. Even more euphoric was Korea's victory in the women's doubles of the inaugural table tennis event.

6

7

8

9

Yang Young-ja and Hyun Jung-hwa scored a spectacular win over the formidable Chinese Republic pair, Jiao Zhimin and Chen Jing. The Koreans went ahead 21-19, lost the second 21-16, but outplayed their opponents to take the final game 21-10. In the women's hockey final, the exciting young Korean team had to give best to Australia, who won by two goals to nil. Gyulay Zsolt of Hungary won the men's kayak singles 500 meters at the Regatta Course, where the GDR took two of the six events decided. Olaf Heukrodt of the GDR, regarded as the world's best canoe sprinter, expectedly won the Canadian singles 500 meters.

4

1. Unorthodox pose for a bandmaster?
2. Rhythmic gymnastics. Panagiova Sitsela in meditational pose.
3. Skipping spectacular.
4. Bird-like balance.
5. Synchronized toes.
6. A name without a face.

6

4

3

DAY **15**

1

THE GAMES OF THE AFRICAN RUNNERS

T he Games of Seoul will be remembered, as much as anything, as the Games of the African runners: above all as the Kenyan Games. Rarely has there been such a domination of the men's middle distance events by one country, wider than the prime Said Aouita through injury before the semi-final, and of Abdi Bile of Somalia, the world champion, before the Games opened. Yet for the bronze by Herold, inches dividing them. It had to be asked whether, over the past four seasons, Cram and Aouita had not raced themselves dry in pursuit of Grand Prix prizes and records. For both of them, Seoul was a sharp reverse. Rono's time was a moderate 3 mins. 35.96 secs., giving cause for reflection on the wisdom of the British selectors in excluding Sebastian Coe, the double gold medalist.

In the weeks preceding the Games, Sam Koskei, the Kenyan national coach, had discussed with Ngugi the proposition that he might attempt to run away from the field in the 5,000 meters. In the world championships, Ngugi had faded because of a knee injury. Two world cross-country titles were, however, proof of stamina. Was the gamble worth it?

2

1, 2. Flojo prays ... and presses on. USA take silver in the 4×400 meters relay.
3, 4. China, FRG and URS pass the parcel. The 4×100 meters relay.

of the British at the previous two Games. The beauty of the Kenyans is the effortless rhythm of their stride, and that beauty brought a spontaneous response from a crowd at the Olympic Stadium which for some of the time had been pianissimo in its appreciation. We had seen the victories of Ereng and Kariuki in the 800 meters and steeplechase, and of Boutaib of Morocco in the 10,000. Now came, within the space of three-quarters of an hour, the judgement of Peter Rono and the audacity of John Ngugi. The field for the 1,500 meters final was admittedly weakened by the withdrawal of Rono produced the perfect run to leave Steve Cram (GBR), the 1984 silver medalist, battling for the places behind him.

The race was innocent enough for two laps, with O'Sullivan of Ireland making the running. On the third lap, Rono raised the pace and at the bell he led from Atkinson (U.S.), Elliot and Cram of Britain, and Herold of the GDR. Down the back straight, Elliot, silver medalist in the world championship 800 meters, and Herold were pressing Rono; but on the last turn he kicked and they could not answer. Rono sustained his tempo, Elliot took second, and Cram was edged out

After three laps in which to get warm, Ngugi went. Ten yards clear, twenty, thirty: before the others knew it, he had gone. With five laps to go, Domingos Castro of Portugal began to try to claw back some of the six-second lead of the lone, loping Kenyan, who occasionally glanced over his shoulder to ensure he was not unnecessarily burning oxygen. On and on he went, the most exhilarating piece of front running since the vain steeplechase bid by Filbert Bayi of Tanzania in the Moscow Games. Ngugi, however, was not to be caught. He still had almost a four-second margin at the line, with a time of 13 mins. 11.70 secs. The unfortunate Castro was passed in the last few meters by both Dieter Baumann (FRG) and Hansjoerg Kunze (GDR). Paula Ivan of Romania was another runaway winner, with a massive six-second margin in the women's 1,500 meters, in a new Olympic record of 3:53.96. A flashing final leg by Evelyn Ashford helped give Florence Griffith-Joyner her third gold medal, the USA winning the 4 x 100 relay as Ashford overtook the GDR and Soviet Union.

1. *Buckner (GBR), sixth in the 5000 meters, duels with Maree (US).*
2. *Alois Hannecker (FRG), eighth in the discus throw.*
3. *Haiti shot putter seems to have her mind elsewhere.*
4. *Heave ho! Ines Mueller (GDR), fourth in the shot put.*
5, 6, 7. *A problem for the Soviet Union in the men's handball final ... the Korean goalkeeper is beaten all ways ... the Soviets have the height ... but sometimes are breached. The Soviets won the gold medal.*
8. *Plenty of rhythm, but no water. Josephs twins prepare to win the silver medal.*
9. 10. *The two heroes of the Games; John Ngugi (KEN) going for the gold in 5,000 m and Peter Rono (KEN) celebrates his win in the 1,500 m.*

5   6

7

1, 2, 3, 4. *Flach and Seguso have the men's doubles final under control ... and don't need a racket when it's all over.*

5, 6. *The awesome power of that right arm is too much for Sabatini ... a Golden Slam would make anybody smile.*

7. *A Canadian badly out of breath between rounds.*

8. *Robert Wangila of Kenya wins Africa's first ever boxing gold medal at welterweight.*

9, 10, 11. *Hitoshi Saito (Japan) defeats Cho Yong-Chul (KOR) ... gets to grips with Stoehr (GDR) ... and raises his arms in victory.*

1

2

3

5

4

6

STEFFI GRAF TURNED HER GRAND SLAM INTO A GOLDEN FINALE

Steffi Graf of FRG turned her Grand Slam year into a golden finale when she won the women's tennis singles, defeating her constant rival, Gabriela Sabatini of Argentina, in straight sets. Sabatini, who had lost the U.S. Open to Graf, was hoping to win Argentina's first gold medal since Helsinki in 1952, in rowing. Her silver was the country's first medal since 1972. Ken Flach and Robert Seguso of the United States won the men's doubles, beating Emilio Sanchez and Sergio Casal of Spain 9-7 in the fifth set.

Hitoshi Saito saved Japan, for so long the masters of judo, from the embarrassment of failing to win a gold medal, when he defeated Henry Stoehr of the GDR. Japan had never previously won less than three golds in an Olympic Games. Saito was the defending heavyweight champion. Nursing a knee injury, he could not attempt his usual throws, but still got the decision. In freestyle wrestling, the Soviet Union won nine medals in the ten divisions, including four gold and four silver.

1. *Arrows of desire.*
2. *Taking aim.*
3. *Jiao Zhimin serves, but China loses to Korea in the women's doubles.*
4. *Nei Qingguang juggles, and China win the men's doubles.*

182

THE SECOND GOLD FOR URS IN FOOTBALL

The Soviet Union won the football final, the second time they have taken the gold medal, beating Brazil 2-1. With two midfield players, Ademir and Geovani, suspended, Brazil were unable to produce the fluid, imaginative play which had carried them through earlier rounds. They took the lead, but it was only when a goal behind in the second half of extra-time that they unloosed their best: too late. Disciplined Soviet play controlled the early game, only for Romario to score for Brazil after half an hour. The Soviets attacked strongly in the

second half, and Dobrovolsky scored from a penalty after Mikhailichenko had been fouled. The Brazilians protested long and in vain before the kick was taken. They should have taken the lead again in the first half of extra-time, but Joao Paolo missed from an easy position. A lob by Savichev over the goalkeeper brought the winner.

The United States and German Democratic Republic each won two gold medals on the first day of boxing finals, Bulgaria and Kenya collecting the other two. Ray Mercer, a U.S. soldier, won the heavyweight title when he knocked out Baik Hun-han of the Republic of Korea after two minutes and sixteen seconds of the first round. Robert Wangila of Kenya became the first boxer from Africa ever to win a gold medal when he stopped Laurent Boudouani of France in the second round of the welterweight final, having knocked him down in the first round.

Great Britain outplayed a defensive FRG team to win the men's hockey for the first time. A crowd of less than 6,000 saw Britain lead by three goals: from Sherwani, two, and Kerly, his eight of the tournament. The German's handicapped by the absence of their most dangerous forward, Blocher, who had been concussed in the semi-final against Netherlands, could only score late in the game. Previous victories by the British, in 1908 and 1920, had been by teams representing only England.

3

2

1, 2. *A goalkeeper cannot be too careful where the ball goes. Taylor of Britain takes a close view ... and there's tricky stuff from Shirwani, scorer of two goals for Britain in the final with FRG, as he weaves down the wing.*
3. *Soviet eludes Brazilian as URS wins football final.*

OCTOBER 2ND, 1988

ECSTASY FOR GELINDO BORIN

To witness the first four men of the marathon running the final lap of the stadium at the same time, on failing legs at the end of more than 26 miles (42 km), was an uplifting climax to the conclusion of 16 days of competition. Seldom has there been such a finish, with only 33 seconds separating the first four. What ecstasy for the winner, Gelindo Bordin of Italy; what agony for Douglas Wakiihuri of Kenya, Houssein Ahmed Saleh of Djibouti and Takeyuki Nakayama of Japan as they glanced across the stadium to see the glory so

1. Crossing the Han River, Douglas Wakihuri (KEN), Ahmed Saleh (DJI) and Bordin (ITA) near the end of the marathon.

1. On the streets of Seoul — Bordin in the lead pack.
2. You can't beat this for a tan.
3. Marathon runners Dupnai (NGU) and Mohammed (NGR) early in the race.

close at hand and yet so far. What gripping drama it had been over the last five kilometers as the lead changed almost as if it were the 1,500 meters final. In turn, Bordin, Wakiihuri and Saleh faded, only to recover. Bordin's revival was the strongest, Saleh's loss of strength the most distressing just at the moment when he had looked, his face as

sunbeaten as a desert rock, to be the most resolute. For a few moments it seemed as though he would be overtaken by Nakayama, yet he too found a last reserve, to win Djibouti's first medal with a heart-stopping six seconds to spare. Bordin's inner will drove him to the front only a mile (1.6 km) from the

Stadium. His beard seemed to stiffen and fire to come into his eye. Yet when he reached the line he had only 15 seconds in hand on Wakiihuri, the winner of last year's world championship in Rome, when Saleh had been second and Bordin third. In Rome the first four had been separated by almost a minute. Bordin is a 29-year-old

surveyor from Verona. His winning time was 2 hours 10 minutes 32 seconds.

4. Gelindo Bordin shows his relief and gives thanks at the end of the men's marathon.

5. You want to what?
6. Gelinde Bordin (ITA) receives a cool towel from a fellow Italian.

7, 8. A handshake and the gold medal for a job well done.
9, 10. Bordin (ITA) shows off his gold. Yes, but is it real?

CONTROVERSY IN BOXING

On the second day of boxing finals, there occurred the second controversy of the tournament. The preliminaries had brought temporary disfavor upon the hosts. This time the controversy turned in the host's favor.

In the light middleweight final, Park Shi-hun was given a 3-2 points decision by the judges over Roy Jones of America. Jones had dominated the fight throughout, and Park later admitted that he considered he had lost. Jones covered his face with towel in disbelief when the decision was announced. To compound the controversy, the international federation, AIBA, subsequently named Jones the best boxer of the Games. Anwar Chowdhry went so far as to say that the verdict was unfair.

Kim Kwang-sun won the flyweight title to give Korea its second gold

1. *Andrew Maynard (US) and Nourmagomed Chanavazov (URS) trade punches in the Light Heavyweight final.*
2. *Roy Jones (US) connects with a left against Si-hun Park (KOR) during the Light Middleweight final.*
3. *The non-stop action of the Flyweight finals. Kwang-sun Kim (KOR) vs. Andreas Tews (GDR) in a hard fought match.*
4. *Grahame Cheney (AUS) moves away from the left of Viatcheslav Janovski (URS) in the Light Welterweight final.*

medal, level with the two won by the German Democratic Republic, with the Americans claiming three: Jones excluded. Andrew Maynard outpointed Nourmagomed Chanavazov of the Soviet Union to win the light heavyweight class by a unanimous verdict. In the super heavyweight class, Lennox Lewis won Canada's only gold medal in boxing when stopping Riddick Bowe (US) in the second round. Kim, regarded as one of the world's outstanding flyweights, said after the finals that he would not turn professional and might retire to concentrate on a post-graduate degree course.

AMERICANS CONFIRM STATUS AS VOLLEYBALL CHAMPIONS

The volleyball competition came to a climax with the successful defense of their 1984 title by the American Men's team, who maintained a long-standing superiority over the Soviet Union to win 3-1 after conceding the first game. It was the first Olympic meeting between the two teams in 20 years, the Americans confirming their status as World and Pan-American champions.

The individual show jumping final,

3

taking place in the Olympic Stadium before the start of the marathon, ended in victory for Pierre Durand of France, riding Jappelop. He had finished second on the first circuit behind Karsten Huck of FRG, who had a clear round on Nepomuk. Durand clinched the gold medal on the second round, with Huck losing a jump-off for the silver medal to Greg Best of the United States. Durand had been one of the favorites in Los Angeles, but failed when Jappelop refused a jump. "We were both too young then," said the 33-year-old Frenchman afterwards, as he fingered his medal with satisfaction.

2

David Broome of Britain, a re-instated professional, who had won bronze medals in 1960 and 1968, shared fourth place with Anne Kursinski (USA). In the water polo final, Yugoslavia retained their title, defeating the United States 9-7

1. France vs Sweden volley-ball.
2. Yachting
3. Water polo final USA-YUG.
4. Volley-ball final US vs USR.

in over-time. In Los Angeles, they had denied the US the gold only on goal difference; since when the rules had been changed to allow over-time. Terry Schroeder, twice on the losing side, said: "It's no easier to take the second way."

As I walked away from the Closing Ceremony of the Olympic Games of 1988 just before the end, a haunting oriental chorale still drifting up into the night sky, more than ever I was in love with Korea. Confronted with the largest ever Games, the people of Seoul had been the perfect hosts. The debt which the Olympic Movement owes to the Republic of Korea and to Seoul is immeasurable.

The Koreans, it is said, have the organizational ability of the Germans, the courtesy and the culture of the orient, and the sense of money of the Americans. With such a blend, they could not be expected to fail. Nor did they. It is undoubtedly true that the Olympic Games tend to bring out the best in a nation, yet few if any have given so freely, and on such a scale, as did these remarkable people during two weeks: or, should it be said, during the previous seven years.

The worst had been expected by some. The International Olympic Committee had been criticized for allowing the Games to proceed in Seoul. Yet what was achieved by a nation that 30 years before had been almost totally destroyed, that until the Games began had no diplomatic relations with the majority of socialist nations, was a triumph of the human spirit, of the will of a people. It was, too, a tribute to the unifying potential of the Games themselves, too often the target of negative, non-sporting objectives.

WARM GOODBYE

The Koreans ended the Games as they had begun them: with color, simplicity and a pageant of their dynastic philosophies. They said goodbye with the warmth with which they had greeted us, and we were sad to be going. The difference from the Opening Ceremony was that the competitors, flowing into the Olympic Stadium like a broad sweep of the Han River itself, pervaded the scene with informal, uninhibited celebration.

They danced and waved and sang as though it was their show, which in a sense it always is. At times they came close to disruption; yet the hosts, with the same calm, hospitable attitude which had characterized their organization for the past 16 days, met this enthusiasm with a benign smile.

The Korean dancers, hemmed in by shapeless tides of athletes, synchronized with the mood of festivity, until the final, lingering melody of sweet sadness and departure.

THE MOST UNITED

As Juan Antonio Samaranch said in his closing address, these had been the best and most united Games in history. No terrorism, no boycotts, but 160 countries and nearly 10,000 competitors assembled in the world's most visible demonstration of friendship. There were moments when sport was disfigured by cheating, but the determination to rid the Games of this creeping poison was amply demonstrated. The re-assurance of these Games was to see Arab and Israeli walking side by side round with a mutual satisfaction of fulfillment.

CLOSING CEREMONY

"Friendship" begins with the Korean Farmers Dance typified by a virorous swirling step using a special hat with a long streamer. The athletes enter the stadium led by a 150 member team of flag bearers.
The Cymbal Dance is performed with the athletes remaining on the field.
Dancers enter the stadium carrying colorful banners which reflect the ancient Korean concept of fraternity.

196

Members of the Barcelona Dance Troupe perform the Sardana dance of Spain's Catalonia region.
Dressed in beautiful Hanbok, Korea's traditional dress, dancers perform the Fan Dance.

Not the least spectacular outcome of the events of 1988 was the performance of the hosts in finishing fourth in the medals table, behind the three great sporting powers, the Soviet Union, the German Democratic Republic and the United States of America. Korea's progress, with 12 gold medals and 33 in all, is as remarkable as the rise of the GDR twenty four years ago, and makes them the foremost sporting nation of Asia, ahead of China, eleventh,

With the stadium lights lowered, the Olympic Flame becomes the center piece of beauty.

and Japan, fourteenth. When you look around, and observe the predominant youth of the nation, their potential seems unlimited. As 75.000 spectators waved their chongsa-chorong, illuminated paper lanterns of red and blue, at the departing guests, the rest of the world gazed with envy and admiration at the close of what had been an unforgettable Olympic Games.

Mr. Pasqual Maragall, Mayor of Barcelona, flanked by Mr. Samaranch, President of the IOC, receives the Olympic Flag and the fireworks begin.
The crowd joins the show as the stadium lights up during the "Lantern Dance".

Reflections of the stadium during the "Lantern Dance".

SEE YOU IN BARCELONA 1992

203

The Program:

Officially, the program: included 26 sports:

- Archery
- Basketball
- Boxing
- Canoeing
- Cycling
- Equestrian Sports
- Fencing
- Football
- Diving
- Synchronized swimming
- Water Polo
- Table Tennis
- Tennis
- Volleyball
- Weightlifting
- Wrestling
- Yachting
- Gymnastics

- Handball
- Hockey
- Judo
- Modern Pentathlon
- Rowing

- Shooting
- Swimming

as well as three demonstration sports and event:

- Baseball
- Taekwondo
- Women's Judo

In total, 237 events took place during 16 days.

THE VENUES
In total, 34 competition venues and 72 training sites had been used for SEOUL '88 Olympic Games.

TRANSPORTATION

A total of 2,511 vehicles had been driven by 3,268 drivers:
1,064 buses with 1,687 drivers
1,316 cars with 1,449 drivers
131 trucks with 132 drivers.
2,000 computers had been put at the disposal of the Olympic Family with the most advanced information system.

THE GREATEST OLYMPIC GAMES EVER IN FACTS

THE PARTICIPANTS
A record of 160 participating countries attended the Games. A total of 14,489 athletes and officials had been accredited;
— Athletes: 7,218 Men
               2,471 Women
— Officials: 4,800

A TOTAL OF 38,800 ACCREDITATIONS HAD BEEN ISSUED!
During the Games 280 ID cards had been lost by their owners.

FOOD
During the Olympic Games, in the Olympic Village, the consumption had been:
100,000 kg of beef
  80,000 kg of pork
  15,800 kg of lamb
125,000 kg of chicken
  35,100 kg of fish
438,000 kg of vegetables
  33,000 kg of rice 400,000 kg of fruits
2,000,000 eggs

THE VOLUNTEERS
A record number of 93,797 volunteers had worked for the Games:

SO (SLOOC)	1,670
SA (Federal Agencies)	15,760
SD (Gov. Departments)	1,479
SV (Diff. services)	26,028
SE (Shorttime empl.)	2,052
SC (Contractors)	12,407
KP (Police, Military)	10,624
KS (Security)	23,777

PRESS, TV AND INFORMATION
A total of 16,030 media accreditations had been issued for the Games:
— Written Press and photographers:
  3,346 journalists
    782 photographers
    800 technicians
— International agencies:
  323 journalists
  106 photographers 168 technicians
— Pool, SLOOC, IOC, IFs:
  66 journalists
  90 photographers
  77 technicians
— Electronic Media:

World broadcasters	3,872
Host broadcasters	3,600
KBS domestic	1,200
NBC	1,600

350 fixed TV cameras and 420 ENG crews had been used to provide a total of 2,450 hours of the international signal.
Approximately 160,000 rolls of KODAK films had been used and processed in the Main Press Center.
More than 3,500 NIKON photographic cameras and 6,000 lenses had been put at the disposal of the Photographers.

RESULTS

ARCHERY

MEN INDIVIDUAL

1. BARRS J.	USA	338 points
2. PARK S.-H.	KOR	336 points
3. ECHEEV V.	URS	335 points

MEN TEAM

1. KOR	986 points
2. USA	972 points
3. GBR	968 points

WOMEN INDIVIDUAL

1. KIM S.-N.	KOR	344 points
2. WANG H.-K.	KOR	332 points
3. YUN Y.-S.	KOR	327 points

WOMEN TEAM

1. KOR	982 points
2. INA	952 points
3. USA	952 points

ATHLETICS

MEN 100M

1. LEWIS C.	USA	9.92 NOR
2. CHRISTIE L.	GBR	9.97
3. SMITH C.	USA	9.99

MEN 200M

1. DELOACH J.	USA	19.75 NOR
2. LEWIS C.	USA	19.79
3. SILVA R.	BRA	20.04

MEN 400M

1. LEWIS S.	USA	43.87
2. REYNOLDS H.B.	USA	43.93
3. EVERETT D.	USA	44.09

MEN 800M

1. ERENG P.	KEN	1:43.45
2. CRUZ J.	BRA	1:43.90
3. AOUITA S.	MAR	1:44.06

MEN 1500M

1. RONO P.	KEN	3:35.96
2. ELLIOTT P.	GBR	3:36.15
3. HEROLD J.P.	GDR	3:36.21

MEN 5000M

1. NGUGI J.	KEN	13:11.70
2. BAUMANN D.	FRG	13:15.52
3. KUNZE H.	GDR	13:15.73

MEN 10000M

1. BOUTAIB M.B.	MAR	27:21.46 NOR
2. ANTIBO S.	ITA	27:23.55
3. KIMELI K.	KEN	27:25.16

MEN 3000M STEEPLECHASE

1. KARIUKI J.	KEN	8:05.51 NOR
2. KOECH P.	KEN	8:06.79
3. ROWLAND M.	GBR	8:07.96

MEN 110M HURDLES

1. KINGDOM R.	USA	12.98 NOR
2. JACKSON C.	GBR	13.28
3. CAMBELL A.	USA	13.38

MEN 400M HURDLES

1. PHILLIPS A.	USA	47.19 NOR
2. BA E.H.D.	SEN	47.23
3. MOSES E.	USA	47.56

MEN 20KM WALK

1. PRIBILINEC J.	TCH	1'19:57
2. WEIGEL R.	GDR	1'20:00
3. DAMILANO M.	ITA	1'20:14

MEN 50KM WALK

1. IVANENKO V.	URS	3'38:29
2. WEIGEL R.	GDR	3'38:56
3. GAUDER H.	GDR	3'39:45

MEN 4 x 100M

1. URS	38.19
2. GBR	38.28
3. FRA	38.40

MEN 4 x 400M

1. USA	2:56.16 EWR
2. JAM	3:00.30
3. FRG	3:00.56

MEN MARATHON

1. BORDIN G.	ITA	2'10:32
2. WAKIIHURI D.	KEN	2'10:47
3. AHMED SALEH H.	DJI	2'10:59

MEN HIGH JUMP

1. AVDEENKO G	URS	2.38 M NOR
2. CONWAY H.	USA	2.36 M EOR
3. POVARNITSYNE R.	URS	2.36 M EOR
SJOBERG P.	SWE	2.36 M EOR

MEN POLE VAULT

1. BUBKA S.	URS	5.90 M NOR
2. GATAOULLINE R.	URS	5.85 M NOR
3. EGOROV G.	URS	5.80 M NOR

MEN LONG JUMP

1. LEWIS C.	USA	8.72 M
2. POWELL M.	USA	8.49 M
3. MYRICKS L.	USA	8.27 M

MEN TRIPLE JUMP

1. MARKOV H.	BUL	17.61 M NOR
2. LAPCHINE I.	URS	17.52 M
3. KOVALENKO A.	URS	17.42 M NOR

MEN SHOT PUT

1. TIMMERMANN U.	GDR	22.47 M NOR
2. BARNES R.	USA	22.39 M NOR
3. GUENTHOER W.	SUI	21.99 M NOR

MEN DISCUS

1. SCHULT J.	GDR	68.82 M NOR
2. OUBARTAS R.	URS	67.48 M
3. DANNEBERG R.	FRG	67.38 M

MEN HAMMER THROW

1. LITVINOV S.	URS	84.80 M
2. SEDYKH Y.	URS	83.76 M
3. TAMM Y.	URS	81.16 M

MEN JAVELIN

1. KORJUS T.	FIN	84.28 M
2. ZELEZNY J.	TCH	84.12 M
3. RATY S.	FIN	83.26 M

MEN DECATHLON

1. SCHENK C.	GDR	8488 points
2. VOSS T.	GDR	8399 points
3. STEEN D.	CAN	8328 points

WOMEN 100M

1. GRIFFITH JOYNER F.	USA	10.54
2. ASHFORD E.	USA	10.83
3. DRECHSLER H.	GDR	10.85

WOMEN 200M

1. GRIFFITH JOYNER F.	USA	21.34 NWR
2. ASHFORD E.	USA	21.72
3. DRECHSLER H.	GDR	21.95

WOMEN 400M

1. BRYZGUINA O.	URS	48.65 NOR
2. MUELLER P.	GDR	49.45
3. NAZAROVA O.	URS	49.90

WOMEN 800M

1. WODARS S.	GDR	1:56.10
2. WACHTEL C.	GDR	1:56.64
3. GALLAGHER K.	USA	1:56.91

WOMEN 1500M

1. IVAN P.	ROM	3:53.96 NOR
2. BAIKAUSKAITE L.	URS	4:00.24
3. SAMOLENKO T.	URS	4:00.30

C. LEWIS
MIZUNO's Advisory Staff

F.G. JOYNER
MIZUNO's Advisory Staff

No.1

Winners of the Men's & Women's
100-meter Sprints

**These two champions
chose Mizuno shoes
for their Gold Medal
performances.**

CALGARY

SEOUL

WOMEN 3000M

1. SAMOLENKO T.	URS	8:26.53 NOR
2. IVAN P.	ROM	8:27.15
3. MURRAY Y.	GBR	8:29.02

WOMEN 10000M

1. BONDARENKO O.	URS	31:05.21 NOR
2. MCCOLGAN E.	GBR	31:08.44
3. JOUPIEVA E.	URS	31:19.82

WOMEN 100M HURDLES

1. DONKOVA J.	BUL	12.38 NOR
2. SIEBERT G.	GDR	12.61
3. ZACKIEWICZ C.	FRG	12.75

WOMEN 400M HURDLES

1. FLINTOFF-KING D.	AUS	53.17 NOR
2. LEDOVSKAIA T.	URS	53.18
3. FIEDLER E.	GDR	53.63

WOMEN 4 x 100M

1. USA		41.98
2. GDR		42.09
3. URS		42.75

WOMEN 4 x 400M

1. URS		3:15.18 NWR
2. USA		3:15.51
3. GDR		3:18.29

WOMEN MARATHON

1. MOTA R.	POR	2'25:40
2. MARTIN L.	AUS	2'25:53
3. DOERRE K.	GDR	2'26:21

WOMEN HIGH JUMP

1. RITTER L.	USA	2.03 M NOR
2. KOSTADINOVA S.	BUL	2.01 M
3. BYKOVA T.	URS	1.99 M

WOMEN LONG JUMP

1. JOYNER-KERSEE J.	USA	7.40 M NOR
2. DRECHSLER H.	GDR	7.22 M
3. TCHISTIAKOVA G.	URS	7.11 M

WOMEN SHOT PUT

1. LISOVSKAYA N.	URS	22.24 M
2. NEIMKE K.	GDR	21.07 M
3. LI M.	CHN	21.06 M

WOMEN DISCUS

1. HELLMANN M.	GDR	72.30 M NOR
2. GANSKY D.	GDR	71.88 M
3. HRISTOVA TZ.	BUL	69.74 M

WOMEN JAVELIN

1. FELKE P.	GDR	74.68 M NOR
2. WHITBREAD F.	GBR	70.32 M
KOCH B.	GDR	67.30 M

WOMEN HEPTATHLON

1. JOYNER-KERSEE J.	USA	7291 points NWR
2. JOHN S.	GDR	6897 points
3. BEHMER A.	GDR	6858 points

MEN 1500M WHEEL CHAIR

1. BADID M.	FRA	3:33.51
2. VAN WINKL	BEL	3:33.61
3. BLANCHEDTE C.	USA	3:34.37

WOMEN 800M WHEEL CHAIR

1. HEDRICK S.	USA	2:11.49
2. HANSEN C.	DEN	2:18.29
3. BROOKS C.	USA	2:18.68

BASKETBALL

MEN	WOMEN
1. URS	1. USA
2. YUG	2. YUG
3. USA	3. URS

BOXING

LIGHT FLY-48 KG

1. HRISTOV I.	BUL	
2. CARBAJAL M.	USA	
3. SERANTES L.	PHI	
ISASZEGI R.	HUN	

FLY -51KG

1. KIM K.-S.	KOR	
2. TEWS A.	GDR	
3. GONZALES M.	MEX	
SKRIABIN T.	URS	

BANTAM -54KG

1. MCKINNEY K.	USA	
2. HRISTOV A.	BUL	
3. JULIO ROCHA J.E.	COL	
MOOLSAN P.	THA	

FEATHER -57KG

1. PARISI G.	ITA	
2. DUMITRESCU D.	ROM	

3. LEE J.-H.	KOR	
ACHIK A.	MAR	

LIGHT -60KG

1. ZUELOW A.	GDR	
2. CRAMNE G.	SWE	
3. ENKHBAT N.	MGL	
ELLIS R.	USA	

LIGHT WELTER -63.5KG

1. JANOVSKI V.	URS	
2. CHENEY G.	AUS	
3. GIES R.	FRG	
MYRBERG L.	SWE	

WELTER -67KG

1. WANGILA R.	KEN	
2. BOUDOUANI L.	FRA	
3. GOULD K.	USA	
DYDAK J.	POL	

LIGHT MIDDLE -71KG

1. PARK S.-H.	KOR	
2. JONES R.	USA	
3. WOODHALL R.	GBR	
DOWNEY R.	CAN	

MIDDLE -75KG

1. MASKE H.	GDR	
2. MARCUS E.	CAN	
3. SANDE C.	KEN	
SYED H.S.	PAK	

LIGHT HEAVY -81KG

1. MAYNARD A.	USA	
2. CHANAVAZOV N.	URS	
3. SKARO D.	YUG	
PETRICH H.	POL	

HEAVY -91KG

1. MERCER R.	USA	
2. BAIK H.-M.	KOR	
3. VANDERLIJDE A.	HOL	
GOLOTA A.	POL	

SUPER HEAVY +91KG

1. LEWIS L.	CAN	
2. BOWE R.	USA	
3. MIROCHNITCHENKO A.	URS	
ZARENKIEWICZ J.	POL	

CANOEING

MEN KAYAK-1500 M

1. GYULAY Z.	HUN	1:44.82
2. STAEHLE A.	GDR	1:46.38
3. MAC DONALD P.	NZL	1:46.46

MEN KAYAK-1 1000M

1. BARTON G.	USA	3:55.27
2. DAVIES G.	AUS	3:55.28
3. WOHLLEBE A.	GDR	3:55.55

MEN KAYAK-2 500M

1. NZL		1:33.98
2. URS		1:34.15
3. HUN		1:34.32

MEN KAYAK-2 1000M

1. USA		3:32.42
2. NZL		3:32.71
3. AUS		3:33.76

MEN KAYAK-4 1000M

1. HUN		3:00.20
2. URS		3:01.40
3. GDR		3:02.37

WOMEN KAYAK-4 500M

1. GDR	1:40.78
2. HUN	1:41.88
3. BUL	1:42.63

MEN CANADIAN-1 500M

1. HEUKRODT O.	GDR	1:56.42
2. SLIVINSKII M.	URS	1:57.26
3. MARINOV M.	BUL	1:57.27

MEN CANADIAN-1 1000M

1. KLEMENTIEV I.	URS	4:12.78
2. SCHMIDT J.	GDR	4:15.83
3. BOUKHALOV N.	BUL	4:18.94

MEN CANADIAN-2 500M

1. URS		1:41.77
2. POL		1:43.61
3. FRA		1:43.81

MEN CANADIAN-2 1000M

1. URS	3:48.36
2. GDR	3:51.44
3. POL	3:54.33

WOMEN KAYAK-1 500M

1. GUECHEVA V.	BUL	1:55.19
2. SCHMIDT B.	GDR	1:55.31
3. DYLEWSKA I.	POL	1:57.38

WOMEN KAYAK-2 500M

1. GDR	1:43.46
2. BUL	1:44.06
3. HOL	1:46.00

MEN 50KM POINTS RACE

1. FROST D.	DEN	00 laps d. 038 points
2. PEELEN L.	HOL	00 laps d. 026 points
3. GANEEV M.	URS	01 laps d. 046 points

MEN 196.8KM INDIVIDUAL ROAD RACE

1. LUDWIG O.	GDR	4'32:22
2. GROENE B.	FRG	4'32:25
3. HENN C.	FRG	4'32:46
* G: Group		

WOMEN SPRINT

1. SALOUMIAE E.	URS
2. LUDING-ROTHENBURG C.	GDR
3. PARASKEVIN-YOUNG C.	USA

WOMEN 82KM INDIVIDUAL ROAD RACE

1. KNOL M.	HOL	2'00:52
2. NIEHAUS J.	FRG	G
3. ZILPORITEE L.	URS	G
* G: Group		

CYCLING

MEN 100KM TEAM TIME TRIAL

1. GDR	1'57:47.7
2. POL	1'57:54.2
3. SWE	1'59:47.3

MEN 1000M TIME TRIAL

1. KIRITCHENKO A.	URS	1:04.499
2. VINNICOMBE M.	AUS	1:04.784
3. LECHNER R.	FRG	1:05.114

MEN 4000M INDIVIDUAL PURSUIT

1. UMARAS G.	URS	4:32.00
2. WOODS D.	AUS	4:35.00
3. DITTERT B.	GDR	4:34.17

MEN SPRINT

1. HESSLICH L.	GDR
2. KOVCHE N.	URS
3. NEIWAND G.	AUS

MEN 4000M TEAM PURSUIT

1. URS	4:13.31
2. GDR	4:14.09
3. AUS	4:16.02

EQUESTRIAN SPORTS

TEAM JUMPING

1. FRG	17.25
2. USA	20.50
3. FRA	27.50

INDIVIDUAL JUMPING

1. DURAND P.	FRA	1.25
2. BEST G.	USA	4.00
3. HUCK K.	FRG	4.00

TEAM DRESSAGE

1. FRG	4302 points
2. SUI	4164 points
3. CAN	3969 points

INDIVIDUAL DRESSAGE

1. UPHOFF N.	FRG	1521 points
2. OTTO-CREPIN M.	FRA	1462 points
3. STUECKELBERGER C.	SUI	1417 points

THREE-DAY EVENT: TEAM

1. FRG	225.95
2. GBR	256.80
3. NZL	271.20

THREE-DAY EVENT: INDIVIDUAL

1. TODD M.	NZL	42.60
2. STARK I.	GBR	52.80
3. LENG V.	GBR	62.00

FENCING

MEN FOIL — TEAM

1. URS
2. FRG
3. HUN

MEN EPEE — TEAM

1. FRA
2. FRG
3. URS

MEN SABRE — TEAM

1. HUN
2. URS
3. ITA

MEN FOIL — INDIVIDUAL

1. CERIONI S.	ITA
2. WAGNER U.	GDR
3. ROMANKOV A.	URS

MEN EPEE — INDIVIDUAL

1. SCHMITT A.	FRG
2. RIBOUD P.	FRA
3. CHOUVALOV A.	URS

MEN SABRE — INDIVIDUAL

1. LAMOUR J.-F.	FRA
2. OLECH J.	POL
3. SCALZO G.	ITA

WOMEN FOIL — TEAM

1. FRG
2. ITA
3. HUN

WOMEN FOIL — INDIVIDUAL

1. FICHTEL A.	FRG
2. BAU S.	FRG
3. FUNKENHAUSER Z.	FRG

FOOTBALL

TEAMS

1. URS
2. BRA
3. FRG

GYMNASTICS

MEN COMPETITION 1a & 1b

1. URS	593.350
2. GDR	588.450
3. JPN	585.600

MEN INDIVIDUAL ALL ROUND

1. ARTEMOV V.	URS	119.125
2. LIOUKINE V.	URS	119.025
3. BILOZERTCHEV D.	URS	118.975

MEN FLOOR EXERCISES

1. KHARIKOV S.	URS	19.925
2. ARTEMOV V.	URS	19.900
3. LOU Y.	CHN	19.850
IKETANI Y.	JPN	19.850

ARENA VISION

THE BRILLIANT SOLUTION IN SPORTS LIGHTING

Philips Lighting

PHILIPS

The legend lives on.

The heritage of more than three decades at the service of professional photographers. The design that is fully compatible with your imagination, and with 29 years of Nikon lenses as well as the full Nikon system. The strength to withstand the toughest conditions, year after year. The intelligence of the largest computer system ever built into a 35mm SLR, with software designed specially for professional needs. The response, the sensitivity and the control unmatched by any other 35mm SLR camera on earth. And the passion. Yours for great photography. Ours for great cameras that have kept the Nikon image alive and growing.

Nikon
NIKON CORPORATION
FUJI BUILDING, 2-3 MARUNOUCHI 3-CHOME, CHIYODA-KU, TOKYO 100, JAPAN.
PHONE: 03-214-5311 TELEX: J22601 NIKON FAX: 03-214-1780

MEN POMMEL HORSE

1. GUERASKOV L.	BUL	19.950
2. BORKAI Z.	HUN	19.950
3. BILOZERTCHEV D.	URS	19.950

MEN RINGS

1. BEHRENDT H.	GDR	19.925
2. BILOZERTCHEV D.	URS	19.925
3. TIPPELT S.	GDR	19.875

MEN HORSE VAULT

1. LOU Y.	CHN	19.875
2. KROLL S.	GDR	19.862
3. PARK J.-H.	KOR	19.775

MEN PARALLEL BARS

1. ARTEMOV V.	URS	19.925
2. LIOUKINE V.	URS	19.900
3. TIPPELT S.	GDR	19.750

MEN HORIZONTAL BAR

1. ARTEMOV V.	URS	19.900
2. LIOUKINE V.	URS	19.900
3. BEHRENDT H.	GDR	19.800
GHERMAN M.	ROM	19.800

WOMEN COMPETITION 1a & 1b

1. URS	395.475
2. ROM	394.125
3. GDR	390.875

WOMEN INDIVIDUAL ALL ROUND

1. CHOUCHOUNOVA E.	URS	79.662
2. SILIVAS D.	ROM	79.637
3. BOGUINSKAIA S.	URS	79.400

WOMEN HORSE VAULT

1. BOGUINSKAIA S.	URS	19.905
2. POTORAC G.	ROM	19.830
3. SILIVAS D.	ROM	19.818

WOMEN UNPARALLEL BARS

1. SILIVAS D.	ROM	20.000
2. KERSTEN D.	GDR	19.987
3. CHOUCHOUNOVA E.	URS	19.962

WOMEN BEAM

1. SILIVAS D.	ROM	19.924
2. CHOUCHOUNOVA E.	URS	19.875
3. POTORAC G.	ROM	19.837
MILLS P.	USA	19.837

WOMEN FLOOR EXERCISES

1. SILIVAS D.	ROM	19.937
2. BOGUINSKAIA S.	URS	19.887
3. DOUDEVA D.	BUL	19.850

WOMEN RHYTMIC COMPETITION

1. LOBATCH M.	URS	60.000
2. DOUNAVSKA A.	BUL	59.950
3. TIMOCHENKO A.	URS	59.875

HANDBALL

MEN	WOMEN
1. URS	1. KOR
2. KOR	2. NOR
3. YUG	3. URS

HOCKEY

MEN	WOMEN
1. GBR	1. AUS
2. FRG	2. KOR
3. HOL	3. HOL

JUDO

EXTRA-LIGHT -60KG

1. KIM J.-Y.	KOR
2. ASANO K.	USA
3. HOSOKAWA S.	JPN
TOTIKACHVILI A.	URS

HALF-LIGHT -65KG

1. LEE K.-K. .	KOR
2. PAWLOWSKI J.	POL
3. CABARETTA B.	FRA
YAMAMOTO Y.	JPN

LIGHT -71KG

1. ALEXANDRE M.	FRA
2. LOLL S.	GDR
3. SWAIN M.	USA
TENADZE G.	URS

HALF-MIDDLE -78KG

1. LEGIEN W.	POL
2. WIENEKE F.	FRG
3. BRECHOT T.	GDR
VARAEV B.	URS

MIDDLE -86KG

1. SEISENBACHER P.	AUT
2. CHESTAKOV V.	URS
3. SPIJKERS B.	HOL
OSAKO A.	JPN

HALF-HEAVY -95KG

1. MIGUEL A.	BRA
2. MEILING M.	FRG
3. VAN DE WALLE R.	BEL
STEWART D.	GBR

HEAVY +95KG

1. SAITO H.	JPN
2. STOEHR H.	GDR
3. CHO Y.-C.	KOR
VERITCHEV G.	URS

MODERN PENTATHLON

TEAM COMPETITION

1. HUN	15,886	points
2. ITA	15,571	points
3. GBR	15,276	points

INDIVIDUAL COMPETITION

1. MARTINEK J.	HUN	5,404	points
2. MASSULO C.	ITA	5.379	points
3. IAGORACHVILI V.	URS	5,367	points

ROWING

MEN FOUR-OARS WITH COXSWAIN

1. GDR	06:10.74
2. ROM	06:13.58
3. NZL	06:15.78

MEN DOUBLE SCULLS

1. HOL	06:21.13
2. SUI	06:22.59
3. URS	06:22.87

MEN PAIR-OARS WITHOUT COXSWAIN

1. GBR	06:36.84
2. ROM	06:38.06
3. YUG	06:41.01

MEN SINGLE SCULLS

1. LANGE T.	GDR	06:49.86
2. KOLBE P.	FRG	06:54.77
3. VERDONK E.	NZL	06:58.66

MEN PAIR-OARS WITH COXSWAIN

1. ITA	06:58.79
2. GDR	07:00.63
3. GBR	07:01.95

MEN FOUR-OARS WITHOUT COXSWAIN

1. GDR	06:03.11
2. USA	06:05.53
3. FRG	06:06.22

MEN QUADRUPLE SCULLS

1. ITA	05:53.37
2. NOR	05:55.08
3. GDR	05:56.13

MEN EIGHT-OARS WITH COXSWAIN

1. FRG	05:46.05
2. URS	05:48.01
3. USA	05:48.26

WOMEN FOUR-OARS WITH COXSWAIN

1. GDR	06:56.00
2. CHN	06:58.78
3. ROM	07:01.13

WOMEN DOUBLE SCULLS

1. GDR	07:00.48
2. ROM	07:04.36
3. BUL	07:06.03

WOMEN PAIR-OARS WITHOUT COXSWAIN

1. ROM	07:28.13
2. BUL	07:31.95
3. NZL	07:35.68

WOMEN SINGLE SCULLS

1. BEHRENDT J.	GDR	07:47.19
2. MARDEN A.	USA	07:50.28
3. GUEORGUIEVA M.	BUL	07:53.65

WOMEN QUADRUPLE SCULLS

1. GDR		06:21.06
2. URS		06:23.47
3. ROM		06:23.81

WOMEN EIGHT-OARS WITH COXSWAIN

1. GDR		06:15.17
2. ROM		06:17.44
3. CHN		06:21.83

SHOOTING

MEN FREE PISTOL

1. BABII S.	ROM	660.0 points
2. SKANAKER R.	SWE	657.0 points
3. BASSINSKI I.	URS	657.0 points

MEN SMALLBORE FREE RIFLE

1. VARGA M.	TCH	703.9 points
2. CHA Y.-C.	KOR	702.8 points
3. ZAHONYI A.	HUN	701.9 points

MEN AIR RIFLE

1. MAKSIMOVIC G.	YUG	695.6 points
2. BERTHELOT N.	FRA	694.2 points
3. RIEDERER J.	FRG	694.0 points

MEN SMALLBORE FREE RIFLE, THREE POSITIONS

1. COOPER M.	GBR	1279.3 points
2. ALLAN A.	GBR	1275.6 points
3. IVANOV K.	URS	1275.0 points

MEN RAPID FIRE PISTOL

1. KOUZMINE A.	URS	698.0 points
2. SCHUMANN R.	GDR	696.0 points
3. KOVACS Z.	HUN	693.0 points

MEN RUNNING GAME TARGET

1. HEIESTAD T.	NOR	689.0 points
2. HUANG S.	CHN	687.0 points
3. AVRAMENKO G.	URS	686.0 points

MEN AIR PISTOL

1. KIRIAKOV T.	BUL	687.9 points
2. BULJUNG E.	USA	687.9 points
3. XU H.	CHN	684.5 points

OPEN MEN OLYMPIC TRAP

1. MONAKOV D.	URS	222 points
2. BEDNARIK M.	TCH	222 points
3. PEETERS F.	BEL	219 points

MEN OLYMPIC SKEET

1. WEGNER A.	GDR	222 points
2. DE IRUARRIZAGA A.	CHI	221 points
3. GUARDIOLA J.	ESP	220 points

WOMEN AIR RIFLE

1. CHILOVA I.	URS	498.5 points
2. SPERBER S.	FRG	497.5 points
3. MALOUKHINA A.	URS	495.8 points

WOMEN SPORT PISTOL

1. SALOUKVADZE N.	URS	690.0 points
2. HASEGAWA T.	JPN	686.0 points
3. SEKARIC J.	YUG	686.0 points

WOMEN AIR PISTOL

1. SEKARIC J.	YUG	489.5 points
2. SALOUKVADZE N.	URS	487.9 points
3. DOBRANTCHEVA M.	URS	485.2 points

WOMEN SMALLBORE STANDARD RIFLE

1. SPERBER S.	FRG	685.6 points
2. LETCHEVA V.	BUL	683.2 points
3. TCHERKASSOVA V.	URS	681.4 points

SWIMMING

MEN 50M FREESTYLE

1. BIONDI M.	USA	22.14 NWR
2. JAGER T.	USA	22.36
3. PRIGODA G.	URS	22.71

MEN 100M FREESTYLE

1. BIONDI M.	USA	48.63 NOR
2. JACOBS C.	USA	49.08
3. CARON S.	FRA	49.62

MEN 200M FREESTYLE

1. ARMSTRONG D.	AUS	1:47.25 NWR
2. HOLMERTZ A.	SWE	1:47.89
3. BIONDI M.	USA	1:47.99

MEN 400M FREESTYLE

1. DASSLER U.	GDR	3:46.95 NWR
2. ARMSTRONG D.	AUS	3:47.15
3. WOJDAT A.	POL	3:47.34

MEN 1500M FREESTYLE

1. SALNIKOV V.	URS	15:00.40
2. PFEIFFER S.	FRG	15:02.69
3. DASSLER U.	GDR	15:06.15

MEN 100M BACKSTROKE

1. SUZUKI D.	JPN	55.05
2. BERKOFF D.	USA	55.18
3. POLIANSKI I.	URS	55.20

MEN 200M BACKSTROKE

1. POLIANSKI I.	URS	1:59.37
2. BALTRUSCH F.	GDR	1:59.60
3. KINGSMAN P.	NZL	2:00.48

MEN 100M BREASTSTROKE

1. MOORHOUSE A.	GBR	1:02.04
2. GUTTLER K.	HUN	1:02.05
3. VOLKOV D.	URS	1:02.20

MEN 200M BREASTSTROKE

1. SZABO J.	HUN	2:13.52
2. GILLINGHAM N.	GBR	2:14.12
3. LOPEZ S.	ESP	2:15.21

MEN 100M BUTTERFLY

1. NESTY A.	SUR	53.00 NOR
2. BIONDI M.	USA	53.01
3. JAMESON A.	GBR	53.30

MEN 200M BUTTERFLY

1. GROSS M.	FRG	1:56.94 NOR
2. NIELSEN B.	DEN	1:58.24
3. MOSSE A.	NZL	1:58.28

MEN 200M INDIVIDUAL MEDLEY

1. DARNYI T.	HUN	2:00.17 NWR
2. KUEHL P.	GDR	2:01.61
3. IAROCHTCHOUK V.	URS	2:02.40

MEN 400M INDIVIDUAL MEDLEY

1. DARNYI T.	HUN	4:14.75 NWR
2. WHARTON D.	USA	4:17.36
3. BATTISTELLI S.	ITA	4:18.01

MEN PLATFORM DIVING

1. LOUGANIS G.	USA	638.61
2. XIONG N.	CHN	637.47
3. MENA J.	MEX	594.39

MEN WATER POLO

1. YUG	2. USA	3. URS

MEN 4 x 100M MEDLEY RELAY

1. USA	3:36.93 NWR
2. CAN	3:39.28
3. URS	3:39.96

MEN 4 x 100M FREESTYLE RELAY

1. USA	3:16.53 NWR
2. URS	3:18.33
3. GDR	3:19.82

MEN 4 x 200M FREESTYLE RELAY

1. USA	7:12.51 NWR
2. GDR	7:13.68
3. FRG	7:14.35

MEN SPRINGBOARD DIVING

1. LOUGANIS G.	USA	730.80
2. TAN L.	CHN	704.88
3. LI D.	CHN	665.28

WOMEN 50M FREESTYLE

1. OTTO K.	GDR	25.49 NOR
2. YANG W.	CHN	25.64
3. MEISSNER K.	GDR	25.71
STERKEL J.	USA	25.71

WOMEN 100M FREESTYLE

1. OTTO K.	GDR	54.93
2. ZHUANG Y.	CHN	55.47
3. PLEWINSKI C.	FRA	55.49

WOMEN 200M FREESTYLE

1. FRIEDRICH H.	GDR	1:57.65 NOR
2. POLL S.	CRC	1:58.67
3. STELLMACH M.	GDR	1:59.01

WOMEN 400M FREESTYLE

1. EVANS J.	USA	4:03.85 NWR
2. FRIEDRICH H.	GDR	4:05.94
3. MOEHRING A.	GDR	4:06.62

WOMEN 800M FREESTYLE

1. EVANS J.	USA	8:20.20 NOR
2. STRAUSS A.	GDR	8:22.09
3. MCDONALD J.	AUS	8:22.93

WOMEN 100M BACKSTROKE

1. OTTO K.	GDR	1:00.89
2. EGERSZEGI K.	HUN	1:01.56
3. SIRCH C.	GDR	1:01.57

WOMEN 200M BACKSTROKE

1. EGERSZEGI K.	HUN	2:09.29 NOR
2. ZIMMERMANN K.	GDR	2:10.61
3. SIRCH C.	GDR	2:11.45

WOMEN 100M BREASTSTROKE

1. DENGALAKOVA T.	URS	1:07.95 NOR
2. FRENKEVA A.	BUL	1:08.74
3. HOERNER S.	GDR	1:08.83

WOMEN 200M BREASTSTROKE

1. HOERNER S.	GDR	2:26.71 NWR
2. HUANG X.	CHN	2:27.49
3. FRENKEVA A.	BUL	2:28.34

WOMEN 100M BUTTERFLY

1. OTTO K.	GDR	59.00 NOR
2. WEIGANG B.	GDR	59.45
3. QIAN H.	CHN	59.52

WOMEN 200M BUTTERFLY

1. NORD K.	GDR	2:09.51
2. WEIGANG B.	GDR	2:09.91
3. MEAGHER M.	USA	2:10.80

WOMEN 200M INDIVIDUAL MEDLEY

1. HUNGER D.	GDR	2:12.59 NOR
2. DENDEBEROVA E.	URS	2:13.31
3. LUNG N. I.	ROM ·	2:14.85

WOMEN 400M INDIVIDUAL MEDLEY

1. EVANS J.	USA	4:37.76
2. LUNG N. I.	ROM	4:39.46
3. HUNGER D.	GDR	4:39.76

WOMEN 4 x 100M MEDLEY RELAY

1. GDR	4:03.74 NOR
2. USA	4:07.90
3. CAN	4:10.49

WOMEN 4 x 100M FREESTYLE RELAY

1. GDR	3:40.63
2. HOL	3:43.39
3. USA	3:44.25

WOMEN SPRINGBOARD DIVING

1. GAO M.	CHN	580.23
2. LI Q.	CHN	534.33
3. MC CORMICK K. A.	USA	533.19

WOMEN PLATFORM DIVING

1. XU Y.	CHN	445.20
2. MITCHELL M.	USA	436.95
3. WILLIAMS W.L	USA	400.44

WOMEN SYNCHRO. SOLO

1. WALDO C.	CAN	200.150
2. RUIZ-CONFORTO T.	USA	197.633
3. KOTANI M.	JPN	191.850

WOMEN SYNCHRO. DUET

1. CAN	197.717
2. USA	197.284
3. JPN	190.159

TABLE TENNIS

MEN SINGLES		MEN DOUBLES
1. YOO N.-K.	KOR	1. CHN
2. KIM K.-T.	KOR	2. YUG
3. LINDH E.	SWE	3. KOR

WOMEN SINGLES		WOMEN DOUBLES
1. CHEN J.	CHN	1. KOR
2. LI H.	CHN	2. CHN
3. JIAO Z.	CHN	3. YUG

TENNIS

MEN SINGLES		MEN DOUBLES
1. MECIR M.	TCH	1. USA
2. MAYOTTE T.	USA	2. ESP
3. EDBERG S.	SWE	3. TCH
GILBERT B.	USA	

WOMEN SINGLES		WOMEN DOUBLES
1. GRAF S.	FRG	1. USA
2. SABATINI G.	ARG	2. TCH
3. GARRISON Z.	USA	3. AUS
MALEEVA M.	BUL	3. FRG

VOLLEYBALL

MEN	WOMEN
1. USA	1. URS
2. URS	2. PER
3. ARG	3. CHN

WEIGHTLIFTING

52KG

1. MARINOV S.	BUL ·	270.0KG NWR
2. CHUN B.-K.	KOR	260.0KG NOR
3. HE Z.	CHN	257.5KG NOR

56KG

1. MIRZOIAN O.	URS	292.5KG NOR
2. HE Y.	CHN	287.5KG NOR
3. LIU S.	CHN	267.5KG

60KG

1. SULEYMANOGLU N.	TUR	342.5KG NWR
2. TOPOUROV S.	BUL	312.5KG NOR
3. YE H.	CHN	287.5KG

67.5KG

1. KUNZ J.	GDR	340.0KG
2. MILITOSSIAN I.	URS	337.5KG
3. LI J.	CHN	325.0KG

75KG

1. GUIDIKOV B.	BUL	375.0KG NOR
2. STEINHOEFEL I.	GDR	360.0KG EOR
3. VARBANOV A.	BUL	357.5KG

82.5KG

1. ARSAMAKOV I.	URS	377.5KG
2. MESSZI I.	HUN	370.0KG
3. LEE H.-K.	KOR	367.5KG

90KG

1. KHRAPATYI A.	URS	412.5KG NOR
2. MOUKHAMEDIAROV N.	URS	400.0KG NOR
3. ZAWADA S.	POL	400.0KG NOR

100KG

1. KOUZNETSOV P.	URS	425.0KG NOR
2. VLAD N.	ROM	402.5KG NOR
3. IMMESBERGER P.	FRG·	395.0KG EOR

110KG

1. ZAKHAREVITCH Y.	URS	455.0KG NWR
2. JACSO J.	HUN	427.5KG NOR
3. WELLER R.	GDR	425.0KG NOR

OVER 110KG

1. KOURLOVITCH A.	URS	462.5KG NOR
2. NERLINGER M.	FRG	430.0KG
3. ZAWIEJA M.	FRG	415.5KG

WRESTLING

GRECO-ROMAN 48KG

1. MAENZA V.	ITA
2. GLAB A.	POL
3. TZENOV B.	BUL

52KG

1. RONNINGEN J.	NOR
2. MIYAHARA A.	JPN
3. LEE J.-S.	KOR

57KG

1. SIKE A.	HUN
2. BALOV S.	BUL
3. HOLIDIS C.	GRE

62KG

1. MADJIDOV K.	URS
2. VANGUELOV J.	BUL
3. AN D.-H.	KOR

68KG

1. DJOULFALAKIAN L.	URS
2. KIM S.-M.	KOR
3. SIPILA T.	FIN

74KG

1. KIM Y.-N.	KOR
2. TOURLYKHANOV D.	URS
3. TRACZ J.	POL

82KG

1. MAMIACHVILI M.	URS
2. KOMAROMI T.	HUN
3. KIM S.-K.	KOR

90KG

1. KOMCHEV A.	BUL
2. KOSKELA H.	FIN
3. POPOV V.	URS

100KG

1. WRONSKI A.	POL
2. HIMMEL G.	FRG
3. KOSLOWSKI D.	USA

130KG

1. KARELINE A.	URS
2. GUEROVSKI R.	BUL
3. JOHANSSON T.	SWE

FREE 48KG

1. KOBAYASHI T.	JPN
2. TZONOV I.	BUL
3. KARAMTCHAKOV S.	URS

52KG

1. SATO M.	JPN
2. TRSTENA S.	YUG
3. TOGOUZOV V.	URS

57KG

1. BELOGLAZOV S.	URS
2. MOHAMMADIAN A.	IRN
3. NOH K.-S.	KOR

62KG

1. SMITH J.	USA
2. SARKISSIAN S.	URS
3. CHTEREV S.	BUL

68KG

1. FADZAEV A.	URS
2. PARK J.-S.	KOR
3. CARR N.	USA

74KG

1. MONDAY K.	USA
2. VARAEV A.	URS
3. SOFIADI R.	BUL

82KG

1. HAN M.-W.	KOR
2. GENCALP N.	TUR
3. LOHYNA J.	TCH

90KG

1. KHADARTSEV M.	URS
2. OTA A.	JPN
3. KIM T.-W.	KOR

100KG

1. PUSCASU V.	ROM
2. KHABELOV L.	URS
3. SCHERR W.	USA

130KG

1. GOBEDJICHVILI D.	URS
2. BAUMGARTNER B.	USA
3. SCHROEDER A.	GDR

YACHTING

SOLING CLASS

1. GDR	11.70	points
2. USA	14.00	points
3. DEN	52.70	points

STAR CLASS

1. GBR	45.70	points
2. USA	48.00	points
3. BRA	50.00	points

FLYING DUTCHMAN CLASS

1. DEN	31.40	points
2. NOR	37.40	points
3. CAN	48.40	points

FINN CLASS

1. DORESTE J.	ESP	38.10	points
2. HOLMBERG P.	ISV	40.40	points
3. CUTLER J.	NZL	45.00	points

TORNADO CLASS

1. FRA	16.00	points
2. NZL	35.40	points
3. BRA	40.10	points

DIVISION II CLASS

1. KENDALL B.	NZL	35.40	points
2. BOERSMA J.D.	AHO	42.70	points
3. GEBHARDT M.	USA	48.00	points

470 CLASS

1. FRA	34.70	points
2. URS	46.00	points
3. USA	51.00	points

WOMEN 470 CLASS

1. USA	26.70	points
2. SWE	40.00	points
3. URS	45.40	points

DEMONSTRATION SPORTS AND EVENT BASEBALL

TEAMS

1. USA
2. JPN
3. PUR

JUDO

WOMEN'S EXTRA LIGHT -48KG

1. LI Z.	CHN
2. ESAKI F.	JPN
3. REARDON J.	AUS
CHO M.-S.	KOR

WOMEN'S HALF-LIGHT -52KG

1. RENDLE S.	GBR
2. BRUN D.	FRA
3. GIUNGI A.	ITA
YAMAGUCHI K.	JPN

WOMEN'S LIGHT -56KG

1. WILLIAMS S.	AUS
2. LIU G.	CHN
3. ARNAUD C.	FRA
PHILIPS R.	FRG

WOMEN'S HALF-MIDDLE -61KG

1. BELL D.	GBR
2. ROETHKE L.	USA
3. MOCHIDA N.	JPN
OLECHNOWICZ B.	POL

WOMEN'S MIDDLE -66KG

1. SASAKI H.	JPN
2. DEYDIER B.	FRA
3. HARTL R.	FRG
PARK J.-Y.	KOR

WOMEN'S HALF-HEAVY -72KG

1. BERGHMANS I.	BEL
2. BAE M.-Y.	KOR
3. CLASSEN B.	FRG
TANABE Y.	JPN

WOMEN'S HEAVY +72KG

1. SERIESE A.	HOL
2. GAO F.	CHN
3. SIGMUND R.	FRG
CASTRO-GOMEZ M.	USA

MEN FIN -50KG

1. KWON T.-H.	KOR	
2. MORENO J.	USA	
3. TORROELLA E.	MEX	
LAMA B.	NEP	

MEN FLY 50KG-54KG

1. HA T.-K.	KOR	
2. GARCIA G.	ESP	
3. DARRAJ A.	BRN	
ABUSHEKHA I.	JOR	

MEN BANTAM 54KG-58KG

1. JI Y.-S.	KOR	
2. SANABRIA J.	ESP	
3. DANESH F.	IRN	
LEE H.-W.	USA	

MEN FEATHER 58KG-64KG

1. CHANG M.-S.	KOR	
2. YAGIZ C.	TUR	
3. KAMAL S.	JOR	
AL GAFAR I.	KSA	

MEN LIGHT 64KG-70KG

1. PARK B.-K.	KOR	
2. SANCHEZ J.M.	ESP	
3. JURADO M.	MEX	
BAKER G.	USA	

MEN WELTER 70KG-76KG

1. CHUNG K.-H.	KOR	
2. D'ORIANO L.	ITA	
3. WU T.-C.	TPE	
WARWICK J.	USA	

MEN MIDDLE 76KG-83KG

1. LEE K.-H.	KOR	
2. HUSSEIN A.	EGY	
3. WOZNICKI M.	FRG	
SAHIN M.	TUR	

MEN HEAVY +83KG

1. KIM J.	USA	
2. KIM J.-S.	KOR	
3. ALVAREZ J.L.	ESP	
ARNDT M.	FRG	

WOMEN FIN -43KG

1. CHIN Y.-F.	TPE	
2. LEE H.-J.	KOR	
3. MARATHAMUTHU V.	MAL	
TORRES M.	MEX	

WOMEN FLY 43KG-47KG

1. CHOO N.-Y.	KOR	
2. NARANJO M.A.	ESP	
3. PAI Y.-Y.	TPE	
PEJO M.	USA	

WOMEN BANTAM 47KG-51KG

1. CHEN Y.-A.	TPE	
2. HOLLOWAY D.	USA	
3. LOPEZ J.	ESP	
PARK S.-Y.	KOR	

WOMEN FEATHER 51KG-55KG

1. CHRISTENSEN A.	DEN	
2. TAN Z.	TUR	
3. DOLLS A.	ESP	
KIM S.-Y.	KOR	

WOMEN LIGHT 55 KG-60 KG

1. HEE D.	USA	
2. SCHWARTZ K.	DEN	
3. VAN DUREN J.	HOL	
CHEN J.-F.	TPE	

WOMEN WELTER 60KG-65KG

1. LIMAS A.	USA	
2. KIM J.-S.	KOR	
3. BISTUER C.	ESP	
SEIDEL S.	FRG	

WOMEN MIDDLE 65KG-70KG

1. KIM H.-H.	KOR	
2. DE JONGH M.	HOL	
3. NAVAZ E.	ESP	
JEWELL S.	USA	

WOMEN HEAVY +70KG

1. LOVE L.	USA	
2. JANG Y.-J.	KOR	
3. FRANSSEN Y.	CAN	
GUESTER U.	FRG	

MEDAL STANDING

	Country	Gold	Silver	Bronze
1	URS U.S.S.R.	55	31	46
2	GDR German Democratic Republic	37	35	30
3	USA United States of America	36	35	30
4	KOR Republic of Korea	12	10	11
5	FRG Federal Republic of Germany	11	14	15
6	HUN Hungary	11	6	6
7	BUL Bulgaria	10	12	13
8	ROM Romania	7	11	6
9	FRA France	6	4	6
10	ITA Italy	6	4	4
11	CHN People's Republic of China	5	11	6
12	GBR Great Britain	5	10	9
13	KEN Kenya	5	2	2
14	JPN Japan	4	3	7
15	AUS Australia	3	6	5
16	YUG Yugoslavia	3	4	5
17	TCH Czechoslovakia	3	3	2
18	NZL New Zealand	3	2	8
19	CAN Canada	3	2	5
20	POL Poland	2	5	9
21	NOR Norway	2	3	0
22	HOL Netherlands	2	2	5
23	DEN Denmark	2	1	1
24	BRA Brazil	1	2	3
25	FIN Finland	1	1	2
26	ESP Spain	1	1	2
27	TUR Turkey	1	1	0
28	MAR Morocco	1	0	2
29	POR Portugal	1	0	0
29	AUT Austria	1	0	0
29	SUR Surinam	1	0	0
32	SWE Sweden	0	4	7
33	SUI Switzerland	0	2	2
34	JAM Jamaica	0	2	0
35	ARG Argentina	0	1	1
36	SEN Senegal	0	1	0
36	AHO Netherlands Antilles	0	1	0
36	CHI Chile	0	1	0
36	ISV Virgin Islands	0	1	0
36	PER Peru	0	1	0
36	CRC Costa Rica	0	1	0
36	INA Indonesia	0	1	0
36	IRN Iran	0	1	0
44	BEL Belgium	0	0	2
44	MEX Mexico	0	0	2
46	THA Thailand	0	0	1
46	MGL Mongolia	0	0	1
46	PAK Pakistan	0	0	1
46	GRE Grece	0	0	1
46	PHI Philippines	0	0	1
46	COL Colombia	0	0	1
46	DJI Djibouti	0	0	1
	TOTAL	241	234	264

Abreviations: NWR: New Worled Record
NOR: New Olympic Record
EWR: Equals World Record
EOR: Equals Olympic Record

Go for the Gold!

Seoul Olympic authorities went looking for a communications system to assure the fast, reliable flow of information relating to the Games.

Their choice: Goldstar.

GoldStar

Semiconductors/Computers & Communications
Consumer Electronics/Electronic Devices/Industrial Systems

Pin trading is one Olympic 'event going on outside the venues which is likely to attract more participants than all 23 official sports combined.

The Olympic pin fever that gripped Los Angeles in 1984 and Calgary earlier this year is sweeping through Seoul. Korean and overseas enthusiasts enjoy a lively exchange of pins and camaraderie. The Olympic pin tradition began in strictly official fashion when the first pins were produced to identify athletes, officials and journalists attending the inaugural Athens Olympics in 1896. Pin trading as a popular Olympic diversion first surfaced at the Lake Placid Winter Games of 1980. Today, Olympic pins are issued by the organizing committees, the International Olympic Committee and the Olympic sponsors.

*The official collection of the Olympic pins,
Seoul '88*